Company D, Frontier Battalion
Capt. Daniel W. & Luvenia Roberts

THE
RANGER
LIFE:

CAMARADERIE
COURAGE,
& COUNTRY

Edited by Michelle M. Haas

Copano Bay Press
2013

Captain Daniel Webster Roberts' text is excerpted from his 1914 book, published under the title *Rangers and Sovereignty*. Mrs. Luvenia Conway Roberts' text is excerpted from her 1928 book, *A Woman's Reminiscences of Six Years in Camp with the Texas Rangers*.

New material copyright 2013, Copano Bay Press

ISBN 978-1-941324-33-2

THE LOT OF OUR MOTHERS WERE CAST WITH OUR FATHERS, AND THEIR SONS AND DAUGHTERS, AND TAKING THE WHOLE FAMILY MADE A UNIT IN THE AGGREGATE OF TEXAS LOYALTY.

-CAPT. DANIEL WEBSTER ROBERTS

CONTENTS

CAPTAIN ROBERTS

MRS. ROBERTS

PUBLISHER'S NOTE

Good help is hard to find. Sterling help is a different story entirely. Consider the history-making task of gathering up a band of men to protect the vast frontier of Texas in 1874. Major John B. Jones was tasked by Governor Coke to select men of the most impressive credentials to stock the Frontier Battalion. After the company captains were named, Jones and the governor relied on them to select men from the area that each company would serve...typically young, single plainsmen whose frontier reputations were known throughout the community. These were men who were already risking life and limb to defend their counties from Indian raids and thieves—men with big hearts, steely determination and impressive 19th century mustaches. Within the multitudes of brave Texas men, what qualified one to serve on this elite force?

Certainly, "adept at frontier life" would have been first on the resume of each man selected. Logically, a man who had been living on the frontier would possess the necessary skills to live in a Ranger camp. He'd know a little something about the construction of and living in makeshift housing—tents, mostly, with the occasional rough log structure or dugout. The ability to subsist, without complaint, on rations of beef, bacon, bread and coffee, as well as the ability to kill, dress and cook game were also a must. Keeping and maintaining strong horses and mules, as ever-ready means of conveyance, was vital. Vigilant and handy with a firearm—check and check.

9

Their lives in the Ranger service did not differ much from how they'd lived in their borderland communities. But the governor and Major Jones needed more than just men who could successfully keep house in the middle of nowhere. They needed *Rangers*.

Love of frontier life is among the first characteristics common to most Ranger memoirs and was an important part of the service. Writing Rangers often mourned the fencing in of the wide open land upon which they had happily lived and had made safe. They loved the land and, as such, they *knew* the land. Love of place makes a man willing to fight for it; knowing the land enables him to fight well. Both of these traits were required in a Ranger.

The Frontier Battalion was organized to take the shape of a military unit. Each company had a captain and two lieutenants. A man selected for Ranger service was a man who could respect the chain of command and obey orders, to ensure safe and efficient operations. That same man also needed to be self sufficient and possess a kind of independent spirit enabling him to take command of a hot situation at the drop of a hat. In the pages that follow, Daniel Webster Roberts tells us that all Rangers were "generals." In that, he means that he could send a man on a scout or give him a task, and it would be done without the supervision or direction of anyone else. Each man had the discipline and skills worthy of the implicit trust of his superiors. And each man was responsible and accountable for his own actions. Messmates had respect and trust for one another, and could maintain respect for the superior officers with whom they often dined and joked.

The first crop of Rangers, though they wore no identifying uniforms or badges to establish their authority, quickly fixed for themselves a firm footing in the minds of their enemies and of the citizens they were to protect. Friend and foe alike were impressed by the Rangers' marksmanship, fearlessness and tenacity in a fight. Settlers slept better at night knowing there was a new law enforcement arm that had their interests in mind, who had the authority to bring justice to the frontier. They knew that Rangers were loyal to them and loyal to Texas, and could be relied upon without a doubt, to pursue swift justice. Outlaws and marauding tribes learned that it was best just to vacate Texas altogether if Rangers were trailing them…and even then, they had no guarantee that a shrewd Ranger captain might not craft a plan to retrieve them from their new outposts.

As Mrs. Roberts points out in her portion of the narrative, Rangers did not accept their perilous posts for love of money. They provided their own horses, camp equipage and clothing, and were responsible for maintaining the same. Each man entered the force with his own pistol. Breach-loaders were provided by the state but the cost was deducted from each company's pay. Rangers were paid quarterly, each receiving $40 per month. Officers received higher wages, with the captain of the company bringing home the most bacon, $100 a month. Ranger horses were compensated, too, in the form of an allowance of oats or corn and a small amount of salt per month. When the state legislature met, these valiant men would quiver like cottontails when the mail arrived. Would the appropriation that kept them in service be sustained? Would the Ranger force be cut?

In the execution of his duties, a Ranger needed the skills of a pioneer and the insight of a psychologist, an innate knowledge of human nature and crisis management, a superlative sense of direction and a keen eye for cutting sign. He was a good judge and even better handler of horses, and a crack shot. He was a faithful subordinate and a proficient leader of men. He was affable and respectful, with good people skills, but unafraid to kill those who would harm Texas and her people. The hearty spirit and myriad traits that made a successful Texas Ranger out of a young pioneer man in 1874 have been passed down to modern Texans through the generations. No true Texan lacks the Ranger spirit—that of loyalty, bravery and love of home. I hope that Captain Roberts and his wife, through this little book, help to remind us all of that spirit, that we might hold it dear and preserve it.

-Michelle M. Haas, Managing Editor
Windy Hill

BACKGROUND

I was born in the State of Mississippi, in Winston County, October 10th, 1841. My father, Alexander Roberts, came to Texas in 1836, and helped the Texans fight the battles of the Republic for nearly four years, being in many engagements with the enemy, the most noted of which was the Plum Creek fight, which has gone into the history of Texas.

Soon after the Plum Creek fight, my mother prevailed on father to take his family to some place of safety, firmly believing that wholesale murder would be their fate. Father's judgment was waived and mother's love of family won her cause, and they went back to Mississippi in 1839.

During their stay in Mississippi, I was born, making that State my native soil, but father's love for Texas had never subsided, and his turn came to persuade mother back to Texas, where he joined his old comrades again in 1843. I was about two years old when they returned to Texas.

My father followed up the frontier, and I was reared, and almost rocked in the cradle of Texas warfare. When I was a small boy, I developed some very peculiar traits of character, not peculiarly good, but rather strangely peculiar.

We were fond of dwelling alone, to commune with Nature's beautiful work. I had my favorite pecan trees, and would conceal myself under them, to hear the crows murmur to each other, while they were gathering the splendid nuts.

My father's recital of early Texas battles had imbued me with the spirit that those old Texans were the rightful lords of that grand and new republic, and that their heroism should be sustained, and when I grew to be a man, that I would devote my life to the cause that my father so loved.

In my boyish dreams I was always in command of men. My education was limited to the common English branches. As I grew to manhood, I could see that war should not be my occupation, but the constant raids of savage foes upon Texas gave me the field that my more youthful days had pictured for me. I was "put in command of men," and my stewardship will follow. My work was more preparatory for civil government, consequently I was never a politician, but always adhered to democratic principles.

INTRODUCTION

I set out in this writing to record the work of Company D, Frontier Battalion, not for any selfish consideration. But, being almost importuned by real friends to do so, I thought I could tell what I really know to be true in a way that might spin out a thread strong enough to bind together an intelligent idea of the needs of that service, how the service was performed, and at least a vision of the final disposition of the horrid Indian question. Egotism doesn't lead me to say that Texas did it all; but our little part is richly treasured in the archives of our "native heath"—Texas. Our sorrows are there, also, in many a grave not even marked by human hands to show where our brave defenders met death—yielding the last sacrifice in defense of Texas.

I challenge the world to produce a citizenship or soldiery more loyal to home and country. Our oldest citizenship were "diamonds in the rough" and no polish has ever added to their intrinsic value. The great big warm hearts of their sons and daughters needed no psychologist to interpret their spirit growth. They were modestly, and innocently, great from birth. When "patent-leather civilization" overtook them they were ill at ease to embrace its gilded charms, but reassurance came to them in a knowledge that good society came from a good base.

I shall abstain from politics, religion or law, only to give a definition of politics, offered by a statesman, who said, "Politics is anything pertaining to law." But from this I dissent, and offer a substitute: "Politics is anything for the betterment of our institutions of government." Religion is the outgrowth of

15

moral ethics, but Christianity is a different thing. Law is the executive branch of both politics and Christianity, it rather seeks shelter under Christ's precedents. Some may say that these great questions have no analogy to the subject, but a great state trying to operate a government under their power, must have a cause and justification.

We had to meet a condition, not a law, of savage atrocity. We could not apply our law in revenge, which made our case clearly one in self defense. The State of Texas realizing this could only operate a force within state lines. The Rangers were her militia, as the name "Ranger" had no standing in law. It came to us more from tradition, when Texas was a republic, and is dear to us yet. The moral force of its meaning will never die in Texas.

Texas found that the practical acquisition of her frontier furnished an asset to the state, which vastly augmented her wealth. The livestock industry easily copes with cotton, sugar and rice, on a basis of money value. Her fruits and cereals only supply home consumption. Her truck gardening is a big item in supplying all our early markets. And can we claim a modest little part in bringing about all this? I abide the answer from true Texans.

ORGANIZATION OF THE RANGERS

A fter the war between the states, the first Democratic Governor elected in Texas was Richard Coke. The citizens of Texas, realizing that the state was overrun with Indians and outlaws, following in the wake of war, found that the battles of its first great pioneers would have to be, in a measure, fought over again. Not for the independence of a republic, but for the life and liberty of her people, guaranteed by the constitution, and compact of states. Consequently, in May, 1874, Governor Coke recommended to the legislature, then in session, to authorize the raising and equipping of a battalion, of six full companies of Rangers, consisting of 75 men to each company, rank and file, to be placed on the Texas frontier, extending from Jacksboro, in Jack County, to the Rio Grande River, bordering on Mexico a distance of 600 miles, on the north and west of the interior of the state.

That legislature was composed of the sterling men of the state, who didn't weigh money with the lives of our people, and after passing the bill appropriated $75,000 to put the Battalion into action as quickly as possible. The six companies of the Battalion were organized and officered as follows: On the extreme east of the line was Captain John Ikard. Then, coming west, was Captain Stevens, then Captain Jeff Malty, then Captain C. R. "Rufe" Perry, commanding Company D. Then came Captain Neal Caldwell and Captain Pat Dolan on the extreme west. The respective companies were distributed approximately 100 miles apart. Our Adjutant General was Wm. Steele; our Major was John B. Jones. Our Quartermaster was Wm. M. Kenney.

Major John B. Jones was the moving spirit of the field work and directed it almost entirely himself. Major Jones was a man of great administrative and executive ability, and none of the Rangers could beat him to a real live scrap with the enemy. He was the right man in the right place. Major Jones detailed five men from each company to serve as an escort with him in traveling from one company to another, up and down the line of companies. That he endured hardships and hard fighting will be mentioned later.

After we had been in the service about five months having had some fighting in the meantime, our Quartermaster informed Governor Coke that the appropriation, $75,000, would not maintain the six companies for two years, or until another legislature could make further appropriation, the deficit being about one-half of the needed sum. Consequently, Governor Coke ordered a reduction of the force to 40 men to each company, rank and file, which was done immediately.

When the reduction of companies came Captain Rufe Perry resigned as captain of Company D, and recommended the author, Lieutenant Dan W. Roberts to take command of the company. This was done over our First Lieutenant, W. W. Ledbetter, who was a splendid gentleman. Mr. Ledbetter, feeling the sting a little, quit the service.

As I have only contemplated a record of the service of Company D, Frontier Battalion, I hope no officer or man of the Battalion will think that I am not big enough to give equal justice to all. My purpose is to give a faithful record of what I know to be true, and I can only represent Company D backed by the archives of the state.

THE DEER CREEK FIGHT

The first Indian fight in which I took part occurred in August, 1873, which was a little more than a year prior to the time the legislature passed the bill providing for the battalion of Rangers to patrol and protect the immense district which might properly be called the outposts of advanced civilization.

The battle was between a small posse of citizens of Round Mountain and a band of marauding Indians which had committed a horrible murder in that neighborhood just a few days before. This butchery was only one of the many which was being perpetrated from day to day along that long stretch of lonely, unprotected border, and afforded convincing proof that some sort of police protection was imperatively needed.

The victims of the Indians were Mr. and Mrs. Thomas Phelps, who lived on their ranch near Cypress Creek some three miles to the south of Round Mountain, in Blanco County. Round Mountain was a small settlement which was only about fifty miles distant from Austin. The grave dangers and deadly perils which menaced the pioneers will be understood all the more readily when it is shown that the Indians carried on their merciless warfare of robbery, arson and murder within fifty miles of the capital of the state.

Mr. and Mrs. Phelps left their home and walked down on Cypress Creek to enjoy a few hours' fishing. Mrs. White, who was Mrs. Phelps' mother, was left at home to take care of the children. A short while after Mr. and Mrs. Phelps left the house Mrs. White heard the firing of guns in the direction of the creek. She knew only too well the terrible significance of these sounds. A negro boy, scared almost out of his wits, hastened to the house of the nearest neighbor and gave the alarm. The "pony" telephone rapidly spread the report and friends hurried to the scene of the killing. The bodies of Mr. and Mrs. Phelps were found on the bank of the creek, where they had been murdered and scalped. The Indians then had a start of several hours, which was too big a lead to overcome, even if an armed posse had been ready to take the trail.

On the following Sunday several of the young men of the neighborhood gathered at the home of my father, Alexander "Buck" Roberts. Repairing to the shade of a little grove nearby, we held a council of war. The situation was too plain to admit of a misunderstanding. The issue involved a matter of life and death and we faced it fairly and squarely. The one resolution introduced and unanimously carried was that the next time the Indians came into our neighborhood, we would follow and fight. There was nothing heroic in our resolution; on the contrary, we were simply governed by the law of self-preservation. If we remained at home and permitted the Indians to continue unmolested in their raids, there was a strong probability that, family by family, nearly all of us would be butchered; while if we engaged them in battle there was at least a fighting chance that we could get some of them. We could do no worse than be killed in the fight and that was a better prospect than being butchered as we slept.

We did not have to wait long after the council of war was held. Within just a few days the report was received that the Indians were in the country to the north of us and were moving south. Again the "pony" telephone was put in operation and the news carried from house to house.

There were only six of us who rode out from Round Mountain to find the trail and run down the Indian band, whose number we had no means of knowing. In the party were Thomas Bird, Joe Bird, John O. Biggs, Stanton Jolly, George T. Roberts (my brother), and myself. We struck the trail on Hickory Creek, about ten miles from Round Mountain. A short time after we struck the trail we were overtaken and joined by Captain James Ingram, William Ingram, Frank Waldrip and Cam Davidson. This unexpected reinforcement brought our squad up to a fighting strength of ten men.

All of us were young men, but we were seasoned plainsmen inured to the hardships of life on the frontier. We knew how to ride hard and shoot straight. The equipment of arms of our squad was very poor, probably inferior to the equipment of the Indians. I remember that several of the boys had only six-shooters and they were not very good ones. I had an old Spencer saddle-gun which had been in the army service. It was a big calibre rifle, with a magazine holding seven shells, and perhaps the best gun in the squad.

On the trail we found where the Indians had killed two beeves and carried away practically all of the meat. The big trail of horses tended to confirm our suspicion that we were trailing a big band. We learned later that every horse had a rider.

We followed the trail at a gallop when the lay of the ground made that speed possible. After following the trail for fifteen miles we saw an Indian run down from the top of a little hill, from which vantage point he had been spying over the back trail. He was about a quarter of a mile away when we sighted him. We knew that the band must be near and that the fight was about to begin. Putting our horses into a dead run we moved forward and around the little hill.

As we came within range they opened fire and our answering volley was fired before we dismounted. With cunning and strategy they had chosen well the place to be overtaken. As we swept into view and into the range of their guns, we realized that every natural advantage was theirs, but no matter how great the handicap we were there to fight. They were entrenched in a little draw to the right of the hill and far enough distant from the hill to prevent us from using that eminence for a breastwork. Our only means of attack was in the open, from the front. To add to their advantage there was a scrub growth of Spanish oak on each side of the ravine. On the further side of the ravine their horses were tied.

The mare that I was riding was young and badly tired, which left me considerably in the rear when the first volley was fired. When I reached the squad I found that my brother had been wounded in the first exchange of shots. A big bullet had struck him on the right side of the face, grazing the cheek bone just under the eye, passing through the nose and grazing the left cheek bone as it passed out. An inch higher and further in would have resulted in instant death. I asked Stanton Jolly to move George out of range and take care of him. This reduced our fighting force to eight men.

We continued to pepper each other as best we could, the final result in doubt from the very beginning. We could not even see when our bullets were finding lodging in the targets. While the others held their ground directly in front, I edged around to the left, and finally reached the side of the gully. From this point I could fire down the gully and, as long as I could hold the position, put the Indians under a sort of crossfire. I had a much better view and could do more effective work from this position. When an Indian would rise from behind the brush to shoot at me, the boys in front had a better shot at him, and when he exposed himself to shoot at the squad, my time came to shoot.

The bullets struck all around me, but I used the Indian tactics, jumping from one side to another of the gully, with my gun always in position to take advantage of an opening for a fair shot. I suspect I must have grown a little bit careless when there was a momentary lull in the firing. I was standing, partly exposed, with my gun in position, when a big bullet struck me in the left thigh, missing the bone and passing entirely through my limb. The shot did not knock me down, but the blood spouted so freely that I thought the main artery had been severed. By this time William Ingram had worked his way around and was firing on the Indians from a short distance from me. I called to him that I had been shot and feared I was mortally wounded, but urged him not to come to me. I continued to stand with my gun in position to shoot.

Bill Ingram was a big, heavyset, good-natured boy, somewhat easy going, but he had the heart of a lion. It was useless to tell him to avoid danger when a comrade had been shot and needed his services. Disregarding the fire of the Indians, he came directly to me. Finding me helpless and in a condition apparently serious, he went out to the open and brought back his horse. Lifting me into the saddle he led the horse out through the shower of bullets.

My wound was bleeding so freely and I was suffering so much for water that the boys realized that they must get me away quickly. We found water within a mile of the scene of the fight, and from there I was carried to Johnson's ranch, about two miles further on. The only injuries sustained by our squad were the two slight wounds on Joe Bird, who had both shoulders grazed by bullets. Several of the horses were slightly wounded.

After carrying George and myself to Johnson's ranch where we could have attention, one of the boys rode over and reported the fight to Captain Rufe Perry, who lived half a mile away. Hastily summoning all the men available he went at once to the battleground, hoping to resume the fight. He found that the Indians had departed as soon as we ceased firing and gave up the fight. He took the trail westward and followed it some distance, but found that the band had a long start that it would be impossible to overtake them before night. Four or five of their horses had been left dead on the battleground. Captain Perry found many blood spots on the trail where the dead and wounded had been laid on the ground.

These Indians were trailed out of the country by other parties. They numbered twenty-seven warriors, so I was informed by parties who saw them come in. One of the parties which trailed them out reported finding the graves of four of the braves who had been consigned to the happy hunting ground as the result of the fight with us.

While I lay convalescing, Hon. H. C. King, State Senator, came to pay me a visit. He was deeply stirred by the report of the fight. He was one of the type of man made famous by Kipling, with plenty of red blood in his veins. He went from our home direct to Austin, where the legislature was then in session, and introduced a bill which provided for a gun to be given to each one of us who participated in the fight, as a testimonial of the State's appreciation of the services we tried to render. The guns awarded were repeating Winchesters of the model of 1873, which had just been perfected and put on the market. I have my gun yet, and I hardly need to add that it is among the most treasured of all my possessions.

The oftener I think of the Deer Creek Fight, the greater is my wonder that all of us were not killed. We were outnumbered by more than three to one, had arms that were inferior to the enemy's and were compelled to fight in the open, at close range, while the Indians had shelter. I can account for the miracle of our escape only by believing that it was an act of Providence.

Captain Rufe Perry, who is mentioned in this chapter, was the first commander of Company D of the Texas Rangers, when the Battalion was organized a year afterward. Of those who were in the Deer Creek Fight, only three other than myself are alive today, so far as I can learn. Bill Ingram lives in Schleicher County, Texas; Joe Bird is still in or near Round Mountain, and John O. Biggs is a resident of Silver City, New Mexico.

No man in the wrong can stand up against a fellow that's in
the right and keeps on a-comin'.

-Captain W. J. McDonald, Frontier Battalion

PADDLESACK MOUNTAIN FIGHT

B eing almost coincident with our Deer Creek Fight, we copy Mr. James R. Moss' account of the Pack-saddle Mountain fight. The Moss brothers and the Roberts brothers were a team that always pulled together, and we never knew a Moss to balk.

On the 4th day of August, 1873, a party of redskins supposed to be Comanches, made a raid into Llano County, and stole a lot of horses, with which they were making their escape out of the country, when a company of eight, Dever Harrington, Robert Brown, Eli Lloyd, Arch Martin, Pink Ayres and the Moss brothers, James R., William and Stephen D., was organized and started in pursuit. After following the trail perhaps a distance of forty miles, the Rangers discovered the Indians about noon on the following day in camp on top of Packsaddle Mountain.

Concealing their movements, the pursuers carefully reconnoitered the situation and discovered that the redskins had made only a temporary halt to rest and refresh themselves. They had passed over an open space about forty yards in width covered with grass and had pitched their camp on the edge of the bluff beyond, leaving their stock in the glade to graze. The bluff where they halted was skirted below with a sparse growth of stunted trees, which, with some scrubby bushes growing adjacent afforded them a good camping ground. Some of the Indians had lain down in the bushes to rest, while others were roasting meat over a stick fire and eating.

It was agreed among the Rangers that they would charge across the glade on horseback and put themselves between the Indians and their horses, then dismount and open fire. The charge was made and all dismounted before firing, except William Moss, who fired two shots from his horse. Though surprised, the Indians gathered their guns and returned the fire, forming as they did so, in a kind of battle line, in which manner they made two separate charges, evidently intending, if possible, to reach their horses. But they were repulsed each time, and a third line was broken up before they got well out of the timber, under cover of which it was formed. One buck, bolder than the rest, advanced alone at some distance to the right of the others, and without firing his gun, which, however, he held grasped in an upright position, seemed determined to make his way to the horses. He came to within a few feet of the Rangers, some of them firing at him, when suddenly he turned and, retreating to the edge of the timber, fell forward stone dead, but, as was afterward found, still tightly grasping his gun.

About this time three or four of the Indians started up a chant and began to file off under the bluff, the others followed suit, and almost in a twinkling, nothing more was seen of them. On inspecting the battleground the Rangers found three bodies. Four of their number were more or less hurt. William Moss was shot in the right arm and shoulder, the ball ranging through the breast and coming out on the left side. Arch Martin was shot in the left groin. Eli Lloyd had three slight wounds in the arms, and Pink

Ayers, two balls in the hips. It was estimated that there were twenty Indians, seventeen bucks, two squaws and a boy. All of the stock which these Indians had, twenty head, together with some of their firearms, saddles and accoutrements, fell into the hands of the Rangers. None of the wounds sustained by the pursuers proved serious, except those of William Moss; he has always suffered more or less with his.

OH, HOW I WISH I HAD THE POWER TO DESCRIBE THE WONDERFUL COUNTRY AS I SAW IT THEN. HOW HAPPY I AM NOW IN MY OLD AGE THAT I AM A NATIVE TEXAN AND SAW THE GRAND FRONTIER BEFORE IT WAS MARRED BY THE HAND OF MAN.

-CAPT. JAMES B. GILLETT

ENLISTMENT & FIRST SCOUT

My connection with the Ranger Battalion was accidental. That is true at least to the extent that I made no application to enlist in the service. In May, 1874, I made all my plans and arrangements to remove to the Territory of New Mexico, to engage in business. This was just at the time that the Battalion was being organized. I had previously spent some time in the territory and was favorably impressed with the business prospects. I had gone so far with my arrangements as to write a notice of my plans to the young lady who has been Mrs. Roberts for a great many years.

Just before I made the start I received a brief letter from Captain Rufe Perry, who had been commissioned a captain and placed in command of Company D. The letter read as follows: "Meet me in Austin May 10th." I had not the remotest idea of what he desired, but the letter had an imperative ring, so I went to Austin. A few minutes after my arrival at the capital, I met Captain Perry on Congress Avenue as he was coming down from the capitol building.

After we had exchanged greetings, he handed me a document without making any comment. The document was a commission as second lieutenant that had been signed a few minutes before by Governor Richard Coke. With the remark "I guess you've got me," I accepted the commission and became one of the charter members of Company D of the Ranger Battalion. I returned home for my equipment and joined the company on its march for the frontier.

Captain Perry, as the commander of a company which was to remain on the frontier, naturally selected some of the members of the company from the men whom he knew personally. It was necessary to have men who were more or less acquainted with life on the border and accustomed to the hardships. He and I had been personal friends for many years and had had scout service together. Our respective families had lived in the same district and been friends for a long time. I write this paragraph as an explanation of his reason for offering me a commission as a lieutenant in his company.

In August of the same year, Captain Perry ordered a scout made to the south of camp to look for Indian signs. The company was then in camp on the San Saba River, twenty miles below Fort McKavett. Eight men were detailed for the scout, with myself in command. At the end of the first day's march we camped near the headwaters of the Little Saline Creek, where we found a spring of good water.

George Bird was sent out to kill a deer. Six of the other members were sent out to graze the horses about a quarter of a mile from the camp. Corporal Matt Murphy was in charge of the horse guard. Murphy was from Mobile and was dubbed "Mobile Register." Notwithstanding the fun we had with him, he was a game, good fellow.

George Bird returned to camp just at sundown. He was laying down his gun when firing commenced out at the horses. The Indian war-cry left no doubt as to the meaning of the shots.

George Bird seized his gun and sprinted for the horses. I stayed right with him. Reaching the horses, we saw that the Indians had given up the fight and fled, after staying for only two exchanges of shots. They had thought to play the role of surprise party, but finding the small squad ready and willing for a fight, quickly decided that discretion was the better part of valor and took to flight. The Rangers loosened hobbles, mounted bareback and rode pell-mell to camp for saddles. We returned to the place where we had seen them last and followed in their wake until dark. In the hurried departure they dropped several blankets and trinkets. One hat which we found will be referred to in a subsequent chapter.

We took the trail early next morning and followed for some thirty miles. The men found evidences which they thought indicated that we had wounded several of the Indians in the fight the night before. Late in the evening we found the tracks diverging in many directions. Scattering was an old trick which they used when closely pursued. Breaking into very small squads, they would agree upon a meeting place generally remote and always in some direction other than the one they had been traveling. After some study of the situation we "called the turn." Our guess was that they would double back and meet somewhere near the point where they made the attack. That this guess hit the mark will be shown in a chapter reporting the fight which we had with them a few days later. The band was composed of Comanches, about twelve in number. We returned to camp, but we waited in vain for them to come within sight or hearing.

The cunning of the Indians is well illustrated in the point of our camp which they selected to attack. Almost invariably they went for the horses first. They seemed to have a mania for stealing horses, even when they did not need them. When they were not bent upon stealing, they delighted in stampeding the horses, leaving the campers afoot.

The squads and companies of Rangers were compelled to use every precaution to prevent the Indians from stampeding the horses. Captain Perry of Company D introduced the custom of using hobbles and side lines. The hobbles were short chains, with a heavy leather strap at each end and fastened to the horse's forefeet, the side lines fastening into one of the straps of the hobbles and extending backward and fastening to the hind foot. Horses so secured could not possibly move faster than a walk and the Indians never could drive them away from us.

One of my rightly enforced regulations was to send all the men of the horse guard out with the horses. And there they stayed. They could arrange their reliefs so as not to work any hardships, but they were required to remain within shooting distance of the horses.

FUGITIVE LIST

After we had been in the service about four months we found that we would be compelled to assist civil officers in the enforcement of law on the frontier. Consequently, Major Jones conceived the idea of some fine constructive work in procuring a list from each county in the state of their criminals, many of whom had fled to the frontier to hide from the law. This, all added up, made a considerable book. A copy of this book was furnished to each company of the Battalion. Several times we found our "neighbors" were wanted on "important business" in the counties they hailed from. A very accurate description was given of men charged with crime, and that was what caught them oftener than names. Every visible scar, or any peculiar movement, or any peculiarity of speech; taking in the color of the hair, height, age, and color of the eyes were all given. My men got so thoroughly trained by observance that a man's name only counted for a starter for his true identity. They all studied the Fugitive List more than the Bible, but always observed the Bible teaching: "Thou shalt not steal or commit murder."

Our work was constant and when we were after Indians there were generally enough men in camp to assist the civil officers in making arrests of criminals. Some of the sheriffs became a little lazy and depended on the Rangers a little too much, while others were jealous of the Rangers in getting to their men first. The Ranger posse was always ready and day and night was their limit on time. The courts did not discourage the civil officers, but the Rangers were their certain dependance. This was kept subrosa by the legal fraternity.

All our district judges sustained the Ranger work, as they did nothing except what was advised by the law branch of the state. We generally turned over prisoners to the sheriffs, unless it was some bad hombre that needed a safer jail than the frontier counties had. The Rangers were under no bond in doing this work, but each one of them was virtually commissioned by the Governor of the state, by acting under his orders, through officers he had commissioned to do the work.

All the state officers, from Governor down, were our strong friends and supporters. Our success was their success and we pulled together like brothers. We really believe that their pride in the work was as great as that of the man who performed it.

LOST VALLEY FIGHT

This chapter marks a departure from the general rule which is followed throughout the remainder of this little book, in that the facts here set down are not taken from my experiences, nor did they come under my observation. My reason for publishing this chapter is that the story of the fight illustrates exceptionally well the gallantry and courage of Major John B. Jones, who was the commander and guiding spirit of the Battalion of Rangers.

The report which is given was taken from an article written for the El Paso *Morning Times* by Sergeant J. B. Gillett, who was a member of Company D. I know from many verbal reports that Sergeant Gillett's story is correct, and therefore have no hesitancy in quoting therefrom. His story is as follows:

Major Jones had made one trip along the line of his companies to the extreme eastern end, where Captain Ikard's company was stationed. On the return trip he camped for the night on the lower edge of Lost Valley, in Jack County. Early on the next morning, a small band of Indians raided Loving's ranch and stole a bunch of horses. The ranchmen being aware of Major Jones' presence hurried to his camp and reported the raid and theft.

This was just what the Major wanted. Here was a fresh Indian trail, within a few miles of his camp. He took with him his entire escort of 30 men, picked up the trail and followed it rapidly. From the signs, there appeared to be 10 or 12 Indians in the party, and as the trail was only a few hours old, the mounts of his command fresh and his men eager for fight, they pushed on at a full gallop; not dreaming that old Lone Wolf, a celebrated Kiowa chief, with 250 warriors, was concealed in a little mott of timber in the upper edge of Lost Valley, eagerly watching the approach of the Rangers. As Major Jones hurried on, all of a sudden he found himself completely surrounded by this fierce band of savages. The Kiowas and Comanches are given up to be the best riders, and most expert horsemen of any Indians on the American Continent.

Those Indians, on their gaily bedecked ponies, circled around and around this command of 30 men, pouring in a perfect fusillade of bullets, being armed with the most improved rifles. Major Jones seeing that it would be impossible to escape, steadied his men the best he could. Many of the Rangers never having been under fire before, became somewhat panicky, and it is said, that it was all Major Jones could do to keep them from trying to break through the Indian line, which would have caused the entire command to have been massacred.

The Rangers were quickly dismounted and took shelter in a small ravine. The horses that could not be protected by shelter were tied in a small pecan mott near at hand. The Indians circled repeatedly around the Rangers and made repeated efforts to rout them, but the boys had become steady now and met each charge of the Indians with a well directed fire. And many a brave warrior was unhorsed and killed. Old Lone Wolf, in person, made a dare devil charge, to show his prowess, but he met with a bullet from Johnny Holmes' rifle, which took his horse from under him. From Johnny Holmes' delicate appearance, and his Chesterfield manners, you would not think there was a "man of steel" at the breech of his rifle. Johnny was enlisted in Company D.

Lone Wolf seeing that he could not dislodge the Rangers, drew off, and with a few long range buffalo guns turned his attention to Major Jones' horses. He shot down and killed every horse that was exposed, 18 head in all. They had now been fighting most of the day, and the Rangers were running short of ammunition. One of the men, Charles Glass, having a fine race mare, told the Major that he believed he could break through the Indians, and carry the news to Jacksboro, where they could get relief. The Major opposed this, but Glass insisted. The Rangers were without water, and their situation becoming critical. Finally, Glass was allowed to make the attempt. His mare had been sheltered by the ravine. He readjusted his saddle, and as he tightened the cinches, it was noticed that his hands trembled like an aspen leaf.

Yet, he was clear grit, and when all was ready, he pulled his hat tight down over his eyes, mounted, dug his spurs deep into the sides of his mare, and at one bound was out of the ditch, running at full speed for the open country. The boys gave him a military salute as he left. Old Lone Wolf was too cunning to be caught napping, and at once some of his best mounted warriors were sent in pursuit. Not having to run so far, they quickly closed in on Glass, and he and his mare were shot down, and killed, before he had gone 600 yards. Thus was the first blood of the Battalion spilled.

But many brave Rangers have gone to their last reward since then. The Rangers attempted to protect Glass the best they could in his flight, and Lee Corn, one of the best Rangers that served in the early days, exposed himself a little too much, and was hit by a large rifle ball, in the right elbow, the bullet shattering the bone and coming out at the wrist. As night came on, it was seen that the Indians were preparing to leave, and by dark, they were all gone. Major Jones came out and marched back to his camp of the morning, with the most of his men on foot. As soon as the Major could remount his men, he continued his march westward, along the line of companies.

WITH FORCES EVEN:
SECOND SALINE FIGHT

A few days had elapsed after the skirmish on Saline Creek, when Major Jones reached Company D encamped on Elm Creek near its junction with the San Saba River, Menard County. The Major struck camp within 200 yards of Company D and the boys that were on the escort detail were home again. They told us all about the Lost Valley Fight.

Next morning Major Jones' escort were all saddled and ready to mount, when two men whom Captain Perry had sent up Elm Creek to get a beef came sailing into their camp and informed the Major that Indians had attacked them about five miles from camp. One of them continued on a dead run to Company D camp and told me what had occurred. Captain Perry was up at the Major's camp, and I did not wait for any orders from superior officers, but told the man to go flying to the horse herd and tell the horse guard to get the horses to camp as quickly as it could be done. In the meantime, I detailed a squad of nine men to go with me. John Staggs, a young man who lived in Menard County, was in our camp at the time and accompanied the detail. He was armed and took an active part in the fight which followed.

Major Jones' escort had moved out, with a man to show them the trail, and were half an hour ahead of me. As soon as we could saddle our horses we mounted and struck a gallop, taking a course a little south of the direction the escort had

41

taken. I had flankers out on each side, so that we could not run over the trail without seeing it. We kept this speed for a distance of about eight miles when we came in sight of men riding briskly to the south, and near the head of Saline Creek. I thought we had sighted the Indians, but when I got nearer I saw that it was the escort, under command of Lieutenant Best, and on the trail of the Indians.

I thought they were going a little too slow, as the Indians would soon reach a shelter of thickets and timber unknown to Lieutenant Best. Since Lieutenant Best was my superior officer, I put my wits to work quickly to master the situation. He had two men ahead of him trailing the Indians, but I thought them too slow a fuse to fire in time. I rode up to the side of Lieutenant Best and asked him if I might assist those men in trailing, to which he replied, "Certainly, do so." Then I had my cue. I lost no time in getting to them and struck a gallop on the trail. I knew what would follow and looked back and saw my men coming after me like stampeded cattle. I have never been quite able to justify my rude conduct toward a superior officer, but I knew something had to be done quickly. The clatter of hoofs was so fast that escort did not know whether they were on the Indian trail or not.

The trail went down a tributary of the Saline about two miles and turned abruptly up another tributary of the same stream, making a V, and leading back northwest to the prairie again. Within two miles of their turn, I came in sight of them. They were riding leisurely and saw us coming about the time we discovered them, but did not attempt to run. I saw they were going to give us a fight. I had time to talk my men down into perfect calmness. I impressed upon them not to over-shoot the enemy, but rather to aim low and kill the horses in preference to missing entirely.

When we reached nearly within firing distance of them, their commander was riding with their rear file and quickly gave his horse a cut and raced to the head of the column. Facing the men about, left into line, they were spaced at proper intervals. It was as pretty a military movement as I ever saw. At that moment I broke column left into line and took intervals, but did not check my speed.

They fired on us, but I did not return the fire, but kept on the charge until we were in easy pistol shot of them, when I ordered a halt and dismounted. They expected us to charge into them, as that is their favorite way of fighting—horseback.

Our respective positions threw their commander on the right of his men and myself on the left of mine. I did not dismount myself, and seeing the Indian commander make a movement toward me, I met him halfway, but before we got together he shot my horse in the shoulder, and thinking my horse might fall and catch me under him, I jumped clear of the saddle to the ground. Just at that moment he jumped off his horse and we came together on foot. He tried his war dance on me to draw my fire, but I held my gun on him until he would settle down so I would not miss him. Seeing that his tactics would not work with me, he tried to get a little further from me.

In my eagerness to fix him I did fire and missed him, but before he could straighten for position to shoot, I put a bullet in the right place. Corporal Thurlow Weed, seeing I was in a tight place, was the first man to get to me. There was another Indian close to me, shooting at me with the same kind of a gun that I was using. I pointed him out to Weed and he came down upon his knee with his rifle in deadly aim, as though he was shooting for beef, and at the fire of his gun the Indian sprang into the air and flattened out, face foremost. The Indians seeing this, and that their commander was gone, showed signs of retreat and I yelled to my men to charge them.

Then the race began. My poor old horse stood trembling, close to me, and I examined his wound hastily and saw that the ball had struck pretty high up in the shoulder, and thought he might carry me a little further, so I mounted to follow the chase. My horse staggered off with me a short distance and gradually recovered until within a short distance further he was at his best speed again; within one mile I was in the lead again. Private George Bryant was riding the shabbiest looking horse in the company, but he had the blood of a "stayer" and he kept by my side until we reached gunshot of the two rear Indians, both riding one horse. Bryant checked up enough to steady himself and fired at them, striking the hind rider in the back of his head, which needs no further explanation. The front rider still plied his quirt, but his horse was failing and I soon got to him. He jumped off his horse and threw up his hands in surrender, telling me in Spanish that he was a friend.

Notwithstanding I had sworn vengeance and sworn that a Comanche could not surrender to me, this fellow, standing before me in human shape, begging for his life, was more than I could stand. I took his arms and held him there until help came to me. Thurlow Weed was one of the first men to me again. I hastily left the Indian in Weed's charge, telling him to let no one hurt him. I resumed the chase quickly, having several men with me then. (But before I proceed further, I will say that this Corporal Thurlow Weed was a nephew of the noted Thurlow Weed of New York.)

Within two miles further we were up again and exchanging hot compliments with them. We made two more "good Indians" in that round. Our horses being exhausted, and my horse having cooled a little by the check, could go no further. Just at this juncture, Lieutenant Best, with two men got to us, and the Indians being faintly in sight yet, he struck the dead run for them.

To camp, about 15 miles distant was our next move. I mounted a horse, and with his owner up behind me we rode double into camp. Two men stayed with my horse and succeeded in getting him to camp late that night. My horse lived and did good service afterward.

When we arrived at camp, Weed was there with his Indian, and had him at a big bright guard fire. I will never forget how that poor devil looked—just as though he thought that fire had been made to cremate him. Now to account for the hat taken in the first skirmish. It was shown to the Indian and he claimed it and put on his head.

We will now follow Lieut. Best to the wind-up of the day. After a run of three or four miles, he reached gunshot of them again, and shots were exchanged until the Indians reached a safe cover, in a place that they had evidently been making for. It was a short canyon, emptying into Las Moras Creek, and at its head it shelved under, making a big space they could take their horses under, and no approach to it except the way they went into it. So Lieutenant Best would edge around until he could see under the shelving rocks and give them a fire occasionally, but probably with no effect. He, however, had wounded one or two of them before they reached this place.

Dark coming on, Lieutenant Best would not give it up. He sent a man to Menardville, about eight miles away, for help. He and one man stayed there to watch as best they could. And near daylight, next morning, his succor came. But the danger of the Indians having fortified their position so as to make attack deadly from the outside was great, so they waited until good daylight to make it. They ventured cautiously until they saw the Indians had escaped.

THE WIND-UP

Now we will trace this band of Indians to a finish. General Mackenzie commanding the 4th Cavalry, United States Army, had made a scout to near the headwaters of the Clear Fork of the Brazos River, and had encountered nearly the whole tribe of the Comanche Indians, in which he used them up pretty badly. But, having only the 4th Cavalry with him, his fight had just begun. They rallied and pursued him for several days, making their attacks at night.

General Mackenzie had captured the greater number of their horses in the first engagement, and that fact caused them to be more persistent. He also had some prisoners. The Indians tried to stampede the horses at night. Mackenzie was a born fighter and the 4th Cavalry stood for anything he would undertake. Seeing his men and horses were becoming exhausted, he rounded up the Indian horses and had them shot down in a pile. Then he resumed his march toward Fort McKavett on the head of the San Saba River.

When his command reached the Concho River, coming south, they spied two Indians coming to meet them. It was open prairie and their escape was impossible, so they squared themselves to fight the whole regiment. But the fight didn't last long, with no casualties except to plant two more of them. These two Indians connect General Mackenzie's scout with my accounting for the band we were first in pursuit of. As the direction they had taken and the time to make the distance was so perfectly coincident, I know they were two of the Indians that escaped from Lieutenant Best on the Las Moras.

There was an Englishman by the name of Kemp, who had belonged to Company D of the Frontier Battalion, who had gone to Fort Sill and was on the watch of movements of the good Indians on that Reservation. Some time had elapsed when a lone Indian came into Fort Sill. Mr. Kemp found that this Indian was one of the band we had been after, and secured his picture, sent it back to the boys in camp, saying, "This is the only one of them that got back."

We will now follow the captive Indian to his end. Next morning after the fight, Captain Perry ordered a squad to take him to Austin and turn him over to the Governor. The Indian was put on a pack mule, his feet fastened together under the mule, so that he could not jump off in passing through brushy places and make his escape. He could ride comfortably. When he was fastened in that manner, again he looked like he thought it was "goodbye John" for him. The guard landed him in Austin safely. Governor Coke said he was a state prisoner, but the expense of keeping him did not belong to any one county and he sent him to the state prison at Huntsville. He was not required to work and only held there for safekeeping. He found company there in the person of old Santana, who was sent there for some horrible murders on our frontier. The old chief recognized him readily and said he was 23 years old and his name was Little Bull of the Comanche tribe.

Little Bull got fat and saucy, but two years of confinement was too much for him and he died of consumption. He was held with a view of a probable exchange for some of our own unfortunate prisoners. This ends that raid by the Indians.

The conditions on the frontier of Texas at that time is why the Frontier Battalion was put in the service of the State. The Indian Bureau, though, was put into the hands and management of a Quaker policy, as it was called, and sentiment ruled

it more than proper executive ability. Fennimore Cooper's
"noble red man" seemed to be the leading spirit of sympathy
and the dastardly murders of our people were readily forgiven
on that score.

There was a bill introduced in Congress to turn over the Indian Bureau to the War Department or to the Army. Senator
Coke of Texas spoke in favor of the measure, saying in part,
"You may treat with the Indian, and he accepts your gifts, but
he takes them as a concession to his prowess, and asks for
more powder and lead to kill our people." He added that the
only thing you can teach an Indian is fear. But Senator Coke
did not stop there. He pleaded with Uncle Sam for indemnity
for the money Texas had to spend for her protection, and it
was partially paid to the state. Paying this money to Texas
was an acknowledgement by the government of default in our
protection. Uncle Sam was not exactly in the life insurance
business, but should have been, under the chartered rights
of Texas.

The bill introduced in Congress transferring the Indian Bureau to the War Department was passed. We then looked for
a change for the better, but I am sorry to say that only a few of
the regular army officers got out of the Rip Van Winkle column. However, I will mention two who did excellent work on
the Texas frontier. They were General Mackenzie and Captain
Bullis.

...WE SEE HIM IN HIS PROPER SETTING, A MAN STANDING ALONE BETWEEN SOCIETY AND ITS ENEMIES.

-WALTER PRESCOTT WEBB, *THE TEXAS RANGERS*

THIRD SALINE FIGHT

A bout the last of November, in 1874, I moved our camp south 15 or 20 miles, to the Little Saline Creek in Mason County and made winter quarters there.

Early one morning in December, Mr. Moore, a ranchman, came to my camp and informed me that the night just past the Indians had stolen all their horses, passing out in a northerly direction. I was not well that morning, but quickly detailed a scout to follow them, Sergeant N. O. Reynolds in charge of scout. Sergeant Reynolds struck west to get the trail and in eight miles from camp he came upon the trail, going north.

On account of the very heavy rains just before this he had no trouble to follow the trail. Within ten miles from where they struck the trail they came in sight of the Indians. The Indians numbered about ten and the scouts about eight. The Indians were hard to beat in management and were very quick to act. They were some distance from the scout, and the ground being very boggy, they started on a retreat but at slow speed. The distance between the scout and the Indians was about a mile. The Indians no doubt expected the scout would cover the distance as quickly as possible and break down their horses in doing so. And that was practically the result.

But three of my men were mounted on good, big Spanish horses that held their speed and kept the interval closed about the same for five or six miles, through the mud nearly knee deep, when my boys discovered the Indians' horses were weakening. Then a fight was in order. My men knew that help was impossible, as they had left all the others early in the chase. James Hawkins, John Cupp and William Springer were the men who overtook them. They determined to fight it out if not one of them ever returned to camp. So, very soon, the firing commenced.

The country was open, practically a prairie. The Indians tried a flank movement on them several times in order to surround them, but my men caught the move in time and would give back a little, breaking their strength in the center and they could easily take care of the flankers. So, this went on, probably two hours. My men had the best of it in horses, as their horses were strong, on grain, and the Indian's horses were grass fed. During the fight my men got two of them down for good, and saw them drag off another one with a rope attached to a horse, which was the only horse they got away with. None of my boys were hurt. After a little relax from excitement and fatigue the Rangers began to gather up their horses and spoils of battle, returning to camp late in the night.

Sergeant Reynolds had come into camp late in the evening and reported the last he had seen of the three men they were still in pursuit of the Indians. At nightfall everything in camp was deathly still. You could see men in little groups discussing in a low voice what might have befallen Jim Hawkins, Cupp and Springer. Some were listening for sounds of hoofs or any token of their approach. Finally one man said he heard the sound of horses coming, and human voices, and still all was anxiety. When they came up to the corral one of them sung out "All's well." Then the yell in camp went up which paid for all our anxiety.

If we may claim any credit for service in the Frontier Battalion, we are inclined to give it to the brave men who did the fighting, at least, in a great measure. They were all Generals.

When we detailed a man to go anywhere to make an arrest or do any particular work, we didn't have to send another man with him to tell him what to do.

My men had lost their pack mule in the fight. As they were so busy looking after their own hair just then, the mule had to take care of itself. When they rounded up the remains of the battle and started for camp the mule was missing. It had followed them by sight or trailed them in the long chase, and soon after they engaged the Indians the mule was with them. The next morning I took four men with me and went to the battleground, and took the mule's trail, which led me up on a little ridge or raise of ground, where the Indians had made their first stand. The mule's trail led me directly to where one of the Indians lay dead, and I could see along the trail and nearby this dead Indian where he had tried to catch the mule, but failed; every track showed plainly in the mud. The trail of the mule led north from there, and within five miles, came to the Las Moras Creek which led east to Menardville and landed in one of my old camps safely with her pack. The people there were uneasy, as they knew the mule and thought something serious had happened to us. We hurried to catch up with the mule, but knew she was safe from the lead of her trail. I had been reported killed once before that, but I knew it was not true when I heard it.

Our pack mules in the service displayed almost human intelligence and were our faithful friends. When we lost our pack mule in the Staked Plains Fight, it was not regretted as merely the loss of a mule, but with sorrow for the poor mule's sake. It was late when we got our mule at Menardville, and slushy snow and mud being bad we camped there that night and returned to camp on the Saline the next day, the distance being 25 miles.

Old Company D turned out five captains of companies, who served in the Frontier Battalion after Captain Perry who was its first commander. They were respectively, Captain D. W. Roberts, Captain L. P. Sieker, Captain N. O. Reynolds, Captain C. L. Neville and Captain Frank Jones. Captain Roberts gave the last four named their first non-commissioned offices.

MOVED CAMP TO LAS MORAS

About the first of June in 1875, I moved camp to Las Moras Creek, being north of my Little Saline camp about twenty miles, and four miles east of the town of Menardville. By this time the citizens had learned that we were good neighbors and began to fall into line. They could see the gleam of hope and our presence cheered them. They could see that they would become the rightful lords of that beautiful country. They would ride to the camp from many miles away, no matter how dark the night, to give me information regarding Indians or outlaws. I had become acquainted with some young men in the country there that wanted to help us and when opportunity offered I would enlist them in the service. They were mostly cattlemen and their range riding was many miles around the ranches. This gave me a prestige in their knowing of every water hole and spring of water in all the arid region adjoining the Staked Plains.

The people began to find out that this was a citizen soldiery, organized under the same power that puts our militia in the field and the Ranger felt that his backing was from the State of Maine to California and from Canada to the most southern point in Texas. He felt that he had very distinguished relatives, from Uncle Sam to our big cousins, the States, and he was ordered and disciplined accordingly. The name, Ranger, was born in the Republic of Texas when great men were on guard for the welfare of their young venture. They may have done some things under emergency that lent a little romance to the name, which yet seems to attach to the name Ranger. When Texas was admitted into the sisterhood of States, the name Ranger was tacitly incorporated into her constitution, meaning her militia.

As time passed on, our neighbors began to think that the Rangers were decent fellows. Some of the Rangers were graduates from the best schools in the country. But their Ranger education was along different lines. They had learned to cope with the Wild Bills and bad men from Bitter Creek. The young ladies and gentlemen began to visit us in camp and the girls would eat beans with us at the mess tables. The Rangers viewed them as beautiful messengers of peace. We could see that social conditions were improving; in a short time you could see some of the boys with standing collars on. Think of it, a Ranger with a standing collar on. They began to name each other—Society Jake, 400 Jim, Ward McAllister, Oscar Wilde, and the like. When they were fitting out for a *baile* (dance) you could see a fellow rustling all the tents for a suit of clothes and the other fellows threatening to follow him and tell who the clothes belonged to.

About that time the racket dance was introduced and they practiced it in camp, in the literal sense of the word. The Rangers made up an amateur troupe and secured some of DeWitt's light draft plays, which they could execute with credit before any kind of an audience. We had a very good string band. Such were the pleasure hours of Ranger life. They nearly all became good cooks and when dinner was ready you could hear some fellow sing out from his mess table, "Delmonico, walloping good truck." We had fish when we wanted them, and all kinds of wild game. When we packed a mule for a scout we invariably tied a chopping axe on the pack to cut bee trees, and had all the honey we could say grace over.

Where is the country on this continent that Texas once was? Echo answers—where? The answer may come that agriculture and other great improvements makes her first. But, shorn of nature's wealth, she only becomes a competitor with other states.

A little while after I had moved camp to Las Moras I got a telegram from Adjutant General Steele, from headquarters at Austin, "To go to Colorado City as quickly as the stage could take me there; travel day and night." The meaning of this was that Captain Marsh's Rangers had killed a "cattleman" by the name of Patterson and telegrams were flying to Austin, "that a citizen had been shot down in cold blood." Colorado City was then a town of tents at the end of the Texas Pacific Railroad, in its construction. I got there and said nothing about my business until I could find out the truth of what had happened. I went to A. W. Dunn & Co., merchants there, and "felt of them softly." When I found out that they were non-partisan and were not mixed up in it in any way, from them I got a start to investigate. They sent me to the railroad agent, Mr. Stocking, and Mr. Stocking showed me the bullet holes shot through his car by Mr. Patterson and others while his family was in the car.

I felt a delicacy in invading Captain Marsh's headquarters on such business, but I was under orders. I met Captain Marsh in the meantime and told him my business. He was very glad to see me there and more than glad, as it relieved him of embarrassment.

Mr. Patterson, while under the influence of liquor, had made some very disparaging remarks about the Rangers and emphasized them with sulphurous language. Captain Marsh had but one arm, having lost one in the Confederate Army. But the arm he had was game to the shoulder and he lit into

Patterson, when a good fisticuff followed. This somewhat disqualified Captain Marsh to deal with what followed. Mr. Patterson was a well-to-do ranchman, and said to be a good man when not under bad influences. The town was full of cow punchers and bad men and women, and they egged Patterson on to defy the law. Three Rangers were detailed to keep order in the town. Mr. Patterson was disturbing the peace and was armed, and the Rangers arrested him several times, and would take him before the justice of the peace and that dignitary would turn him loose by fining him one dollar. The Rangers told Patterson that they would kill him if he didn't stop it. So he persisted in painting the town red and they did kill him. I made my report to the Adjutant General, according to the facts, and returned to my own company.

THE STAKED PLAINS FIGHT

In August, 1875, a band of Indians came down into Kimble, Mason and Menard counties, entering Kimble County first, then east into Mason, and out north through Menard County. Near the line of Kimble and Mason Counties stood a little flat-topped mountain, overlooking the Kimble and Mason road. Those Indians had two prisoners with them, one was a white boy named Fisher, whom they had captured in Mason County when he was quite young, and the other one was a Mexican boy that they had captured in Uvalde County. Both had grown up to be nearly men.

The Indians left these two boys on top of the little mountain to spy out on the road for any passers, or pursuers, while they diverged south, into Major Seth Mabry's pasture, to collect horses. While those boys were on top of the mountain, at their post, C. C. Smith and another cattleman came along the road. The white boy, Fisher, proposed to the Mexican, that they go down and kill them, but the Mexican wouldn't agree to it. I knew all this by my capturing the Mexican later, and getting his own story in broken Spanish, his having almost lost his mother tongue from long Indian captivity.

I was then encamped on the Las Moras, about 50 miles north of where they were raiding. A messenger came to my camp from Mason County and informed me of the raid, and told me where they were last seen, and the way they were headed coming out. I had no time to lose, as I knew they would travel at night. I started east with eight men and within 12 miles came upon their trail. I had no trouble to follow it, as they had stolen a big lot of horses. I pushed ahead on their trail, hoping to catch them before night, but they had too much time on me, and nightfall caught me, just where they crossed the Fort McKavett and Concho road. I looked ahead, in their direction, and could see the little Lipan Mountains on the head of the South Concho, and I figured they would rest there, where they could spy back on their trail.

I turned north, on the Concho road, and traveled that night to Kickapoo Springs, where I could get horseshoes, my horse having cast two of his shoes that day, and broken his hoofs, so that he was almost past shoeing. We shod up, by firelight, and were riding by daylight, north, on the Concho road, with flankers on either side, so we would cross no trails without seeing them. We came to Lipan Springs, 15 or 20 miles from Kickapoo, and from Lipan, we bore northwest completely surrounding the Lipan Mountains. On that day's march I rode upon a rattler and got my horse snake-bitten. I changed off to a pack mule, but I knew the mule and knew she was a dandy, and could run like a red fox. I left a man with my horse, to get him back to Lipan Springs and take care of him.

We reached Wash DeLong's camp that night, on the head of South Concho, where he was taking out an irrigation ditch. Wash was an old-timer, and had been shot and maimed by the Indians, but still insisted on living where he pleased. He gave me considerable information, as to their pass-ways, in and out.

Next morning I bore a little south of west, to catch their trail, after their passing through the Lipan Mountains. About 18 miles from DeLong's camp, I came upon the Indian camp, where they had left that morning. Then the race for that day began. They skirted the head brakes of the Conchos, and night caught me again, where they had reached a high table land, known as the Staked Plains. I was very close to them at night.

I pulled a little off of the trail, and wouldn't let a man strike a match to smoke, as they could see a light a long distance in that country. By daylight I was in the saddle, and going on the trail. I had field glasses, and occasionally would look for them, but one Ranger's eyes beat my glasses. He sung out "Yonder they are!" and I put my glasses on his object and saw them plainly. They were just moving out from their camp, at a big lake of water, which was unknown to many white men. The Mexican told me afterwards that one of them said, as they moved out from camp, that no white man would ever come there, and if they did he could whip ten of them. So, you see, the red man is not immune from braggadocio. It was not an hour until he had a test of it.

Now, to get them, in that open plain. The sun was just up good, and put on his big blaze for an August day. The direction they were from us, nearly lined them with the sun, and I ordered my men to line in straight behind me, in single file, which would only show a breast of one man. They did, and tracked as plumb as a new wagon. I got nearly in shooting distance of those fellows before they saw me. Two of the Indians were loitering along behind the main squad, who were driving the horses and about two hundred yards behind them, and we could have shot them before they saw us, but we didn't want to flush the main bunch, until we could get near enough to do business. When the two Indians saw us, it was a very busy time with them. They plied their quirts, and yelled to their comrades, and we were not losing any time or distance on them. When Indians are driving a herd of stolen horses, they leave drag ropes to the best horses, as an "emergency clause." In this case, they barely had time to jump down, grab ropes and change horses, which some of them did, leaving their saddles on the horses they had so unceremoniously quit.

They ran out, into line and squared themselves for the charge. I played my old ruse on them. We ran up close enough to do good work, halted, and dismounted. I always figured that one good man on the ground with a gun in his hands was worth three in the saddle. They stood one good round, and began to smell blood and left there, like a covey of quail. There was one Indian riding ahead of them, about a half a mile, who had not seen or heard any of this, and when they got to him, he rallied them and they made another stand, and fought like demons for a few minutes. We were wounding some of their horses, as well as warriors, and to lose a horse right then was "goodbye John" to the rider. One Indian's horse was shot from under him, and he had caught the same bullet through the ankle, but didn't break the bone, and he jumped up behind the young man Fisher, on a big stallion that belonged to John Bright, and just then, they began to "hit the breeze" in different directions.

The commander of the Indians was old Magooshe, a Lipan, now on the Mescalero Reservation and claims to be an Apache. Magooshe broke to the left, with six men, and I put in after him, with three men, and I must tell you who those brave men were. They were Jim Hawkins, Paul Durham, and Nick Donley. Donley was an Irishman and loved peace, but a fight, for him, was a mere incident. The other Indians broke into different squads, and my men after them. We pursued Magooshe and his party at full speed, for three or four miles, when we saw one of their horses weakening, and gradually falling back, and we had fired several times at the rider. All of a sudden, the rider jerked up his horse, wheeled him about, and came back to meet us, and yelling in broken Spanish that he was a friend. I told the men not to shoot him. He was the Mexican captive that the Indians had held so long. We passed the Mexican, with the brief words to Donley to stay with him until we returned.

We were making pretty near an even race, in distance, with those ahead of us, and could see blood running down one of their backs. A distance of about two miles further, our own horses began to weaken, and we could see a little clump of mesquite brush that the Indians were making for. One of them was riding a fine horse that belonged to Rans Moore, and when we got near the brush we could see a horse tied in there. We sheared around on either side of the brush, but could see no Indians in there. We looked ahead and saw them still going. We pursued them, but never could get much closer. We could see, however, that two of them were on a big mare mule that also belonged to John Bright. We kept up the best lick we could, until they gradually went out of sight. We could nearly read what had happened, by their tying Rans Moore's horse in the brush. The wounded Indian was riding the big mule and had to stop, or have help. The other Indian tied his horse there, jumped up behind him, presumably to hold him on. He tied the horse, thinking we might check to reconnoitre the spot, and give them more distance ahead of us. The little pack mule I was riding kept an easy lead all day. Don't talk to me about a mule! If he will run at all, and you give him a starter, you will never catch him.

We went back to where we had left Donley with the Mexican—no Donley, anywhere in sight. The tension of excitement was abated, and we could think more about the tired condition of our horses and rode at a moderate gait, to where we had the first fight. We found Donley there with the prisoner. He explained that after staying where we left him several hours, he thought we might never return, and "that dreary plain made him lonesome" (Irish). The other men had all gotten back, and gave the casualties of their respective chases.

Sergeant Ed Sieker and J. B. Gillett had followed the white man, Fisher, and the Indian up behind him, on a dead run for several miles, and seeing they were outrunning them, both on one horse, Gillett jumped off his horse, took a long shot at them and struck their horse, just back of the ears, when he fell like a ton of brick. They ran up to the horse, and found Fisher pinioned under him, and Gillett told Sieker not to shoot him, that he was a white man. The Indian rolled off when the horse fell, and dodged around a while, but they soon got him. When they went back to look after Fisher, he had worked himself from under the horse and was gone. They thought he couldn't escape in that open plain. The grass was high and that was the only shelter. When they told me what they could about it, I sent them back to see if they could find him. Then the sun was about an hour high, and didn't give much time to hunt him. They returned, at dusk, without finding him.

We found then that we had nothing to eat, having lost our pack mule in the race. We had not stopped the day before to cook anything and were feeling like a lot of hoboes on a western railroad. We had captured a big lot of mustang meat from the Indians, but it was only barbecued enough to make it palatable for a buzzard, and the boys only sampled it lightly. It was about 70 miles back the nearest way to Wash DeLong's camp on the head of South Concho, and we had a herd of broken down horses to drive. It took us nearly two days to get into DeLong's camp. Some of the boys tried prickly pear apples, but it didn't take long to get all of them that were good. When we got within ten miles of Mr. DeLong's camp, I took the Mexican with me, and hurried on to have a beef killed and get something for the men to eat. Arriving at the camp, I found Mr. DeLong was not there, but that fact didn't bother me much. I went into his little cabin, found some big pans full of sweet milk, and drank milk like a hungry porker, and gave the Mexican his fill of it. Mr. DeLong soon came in, and we had a spread for the Rangers that tasted superior to anything that Delmonico's ever served.

I will tell you later, all about Fisher. Next day, we started for camp on Las Moras, (meaning morass, or marshy) a distance of about a hundred miles, but we were safe for grub. All the frontiersmen made the Rangers as welcome as the flowers in May, besides we were getting back to our backing, by the great state of Texas. A few days after we got to camp, Major Jones arrived there. We turned the Mexican over to him, and as we had not heard of his people directly, the Major thought he would keep the Mexican with him, until we could locate his people. The newspapers had given publicity to our having him, and his people came from Uvalde County and got him.

Now, to account for Fisher. Nearly a year after this, Fisher was found, at Fort Sill, with the Indians, and parties negotiated for him, or rather, his liberty, and sent him back to his people, in Mason County, Texas. Think of it—to buy one of our captive people, from a savage tribe who were seeking shelter under our government.

I saw Fisher after he came back, and had a talk with him. He told me that he was back on the identical ground where the horse was shot from under him, and could tell me of the incidents that occurred in that fight, that I had forgotten. He told me that when the men were hunting for him in the grass, that they had ridden very close to him, but he was hugging the ground. I asked him why he didn't show himself, and he said he thought they would kill him. Fisher visits the same old squad of Indians occasionally, on the Mescalero Reservation.

Viewing Out A Road

Within six weeks after our Staked Plains skirmish our Adjutant General, Wm. Steele, received a requisition from Colonel Klitz, commanding the post at Fort McKavett, asking for a man to go with a detachment of U. S. soldiers to view out a road from Fort McKavett to Fort Stockton. Fort McKavett was at the head springs of the San Saba River, and Fort Stockton was 26 miles west of the Pecos River, and opposite the old Horsehead Crossing. The fact had become pretty generally known that the Rangers traveled without a map or compass. Their reckonings were made by the sun and North Star, taking into consideration the main rivers that run through the state, from north to south and the relative distance between them.

Lieutenant Bottsford of the regular army was in command of the detachment to view out the road. General Steele ordered us to furnish the guide, and I detailed Sergeant Ed Sieker to go with them. Sergeant Sieker had been with me in the Plains Fight, when we were led to these big lakes by the Indians, and was as good as a Comanche on direction.

He started out to lead them through. Sergeant Sieker had a keen sense of the ridiculous, and told me of the great praise he had heard of himself from the Soldier Boys when they were lying on their blankets at night. They said they might have all perished if he had not passed them through the "Red Sea." They made him out the equal if not greater than Kit Carson. Sergeant Sieker was enjoying a laugh to himself, mixed with pity, for men in their occupation to be so dependent.

In crossing the table land Sieker rode up squarely to our pack mule that we had lost in the engagement with the Indians. The poor mule was dead, and the pack lying with it. He thought if the Rangers had been with him, they would have buried it with the honors of war.

He bore northwest for his direction, and in 20 or 30 miles, they came to the head brakes of some stream, where it threaded out against the table land. It proved to be Live Oak Creek, a tributary of the Pecos River.

Just there, Sergeant Sieker noticed little trails of deer and antelope, which pointed in to one place, and thinking they went to water, he followed the little trails down to a little depression and did find water. The water only showed up about two feet in length, down in a crevice of rocks, and those small animals had worn the rocks slick putting their heads in there to drink. It was fine, living water.

Then the scout was all right, had plenty of good water and could get an antelope or deer when they wanted it. After Lieutenant Bottsford rested a while he began to figure where he was, and concluded that was the head drainage of Live Oak Creek, that entered into the Pecos at old Fort Lancaster, which was right. Then he had easy sailing for his road. He went west to the pontoon crossing on the Pecos, then he had his road to Fort Stockton. That spring was named Grierson Spring, but Ed Sieker found it. Lieutenant Bottsford was a good officer, and Ed Sieker is dead, but his memory still lives.

CAPTAIN ROBERTS MARRIED

About the last of August, 1875, Major John B. Jones reached Company D on his march westward along the line of the companies. He had an inkling that I was intending to tender my resignation, the purpose being to get married. The Major, in his characteristic fine tact, broached the matter first, and in his keen black eyes was a laughing twinkle that told me that he had anticipated me fully. He told me that he was in perfect accord with my idea of getting married, but, that my resignation was not at all necessary. He told me I could have a leave of absence, as long as I thought necessary, and to bring my wife on out to the company, or, I could leave her temporarily at a neighboring village until I could prepare comfortable quarters for her in or near camp. He said he would see to it that such arrangements were satisfactorily made.

I agreed to do as he told me. But, a second consideration came to my mind, that I had been too hasty. My intended bride had not been consulted, as to whether she would come out among the redskins or not. She had been reared in the town of Columbus, Texas, and knew comparatively little about the frontier. But I went to Columbus and told her the whole story, and happily, she agreed to the programme, and appeared to think it the climax of all the romance she had ever indulged in.

My wife was Miss Luvenia Conway, and we were married on September 13th, 1875. Mrs. Roberts is still living, and keeps my good old love letters as a menace to treachery. We took leave of Columbus, immediately after our marriage ceremony, the train having waited for the event, and via the City of Houston, we reached the City of Austin on September 14th. Stayed in Austin a few days, or until our ambulance and escort could meet us there.

When the boys made their appearance, it was Mrs. Roberts' first sight of Rangers. When we took up our march for camp, nearly 200 miles distant, four men rode just ahead of the ambulance, with all the paraphernalia of Rangers. I noticed Mrs. Roberts taking them in, with intense scrutiny. Their broad belts were full of cartridges, and a leather string to which a hair brush was attached (to clean the rifle barrel), which hung down from the rear of the belt, was the one thing that appeared to confound her. Finally she ventured to ask me what that was. I told her that all the original stock of Rangers had caudal appendages (tails). She gave me her first searching, doubtful look. In after years, she found out, that I was a charter member of the Ananias Club.

The second day's march took us by the residence of an old colored woman, that had belonged to my father since before I was born. I could not pass her without stopping to see her. She came out and grabbed me, in the fashion of a silver-tip bear, and pressed me to her good old warm heart. I introduced her to my wife, and her first expression was, "Daniel, you have married a beautiful woman." Mrs. Roberts took the compliment gracefully, but after we had driven a little distance from the cabin, I told her that the old darky had been blind for forty years.

That evening brought us to Blanco City (my old home town), where we were greeted with open arms by some of the best men and women on earth. That reassured my wife that I might have been respectable when I was young. The next day brought us to Fredericksburg. It was on Sunday evening. The custom of the old German people was to have their gala day on Sunday, and a big ball was on tap at Charles Nimitz's hotel. Mrs. Roberts watched the gay dancers, until Terpsicore got the best of the Bible, and she joined in the beautiful waltz. She wished that the dance might last until morning, as she might merge the dark end of two days into only half of a crime.

Next day we reached Fort Mason. Mason was General Robert E. Lee's antebellum quarters. We were then within 50 miles of my camp. I could begin to hear what was happening in that section. I concluded that I had better leave Mrs. Roberts in Mason, and go myself up to the head of the San Saba River, where my camp was, and see if the sky was all clear. I left my wife in Mason, with my friends, Mr. and Mrs. Henry M. Holmes. Mr. Holmes was the private secretary of Governor Sul Ross. I went on up to my camp and found matters quiet. I returned to Mason within ten days, and took Mrs. Roberts up to Menardville, where we were to take our Ranger quarters for the winter.

There was not a house in the town that was in any way related to a saw mill, and brick yards were away back in older civilization. We engaged board with Mr. and Mrs. John Scott. Mrs. Scott was postmaster at Menardville, and she was an estimable lady. She had plenty of work to do besides a pen full of cows to milk. I volunteered to milk the cows for her, but she told me that "they wouldn't let John come into the pen." I insisted that she should give me the pail and let me try it, which she did. I walked into the pen and milked the cows without any difficulty, and I guess John Scott hates me for it yet.

I prepared quarters for us, about one and one-half miles from the town, and we soon went into camp. Here we spent our honeymoon, with sweet old King Nature, watching the wild ducks and geese splash in the beautiful water of the San Saba River. Our only music was the gobble of wild turkeys and the splash of beavers' tails against the water, and our little string band in camp sent a wireless message back—to Home Sweet Home.

The rifle and revolver were not the only potent factors in advancing the successful settlement of the frontier. The "Man with the Hoe," was our partner, and while we watched his enemies, he, in turn, supplied us with corn and oats for our faithful horses, and built himself a nice home. As soon as people began to feel secure in their citizenship, the American spirit of enterprise asserted itself.

When the Republic of Texas came into the Union of States, she reserved all her public domain, and appropriated it to the upbuilding of the state, in public institutions and school funds. And Uncle Sam was not more liberal in giving the people homes. I think it was the Fourteenth Legislature that offered a land subsidy, to encourage irrigation, specifying the dimensions of a ditch to carry the water, say six feet wide, at the bottom of the ditch, and twelve feet wide, from cut to cut across the top, and four feet deep, on level ground. For this class of ditch, the state offered three sections of land to the mile of ditch, not otherwise appropriated, to the makers of that grade of ditches, the state not reserving any rental, or any further claim on the enterprise. Under this covenant, between the state and the citizen we had the pleasure of seeing the first ditch made, and stood guard for the workers in their happy vocation.

THE MASON COUNTY WAR

When we were encamped in Mason County, a feud between cattlemen arose to proportions that gave it the name of the "Mason County War." Major Jones had to take the bull by the horns and help to quell it. The civil authorities also did their best to stop it, but it hinged in the midst of what was probably the largest of cattle operations in the state at that time.

The largest per cent of citizens in Mason County were Germans who had accumulated fine stocks of cattle by their usual frugality. Mr. Lemberg was engaged in shipping and driving cattle to the Kansas markets. He had in his employ Mr. Tim Williamson, who handled his herds. Complaint was rife that cattle belonging to ranchmen were taken by wholesale, by the men moving herds, and not accounted for to the owners.

Mr. Williamson was on his road to the town of Mason, being 15 or 20 miles from Lemberg's store, when a mob seized him and killed him. This act was laid to the Germans. Other cattlemen, who were thought to be shady in their dealings, took advantage of this to excite the Americans against the Germans. This started the Mason County War.

I was in the town of Mason, having come in alone to buy grain for my camp, and was sleeping at Major Hunter's hotel. I had not more than embraced the sweet charms of Morpheus when Sheriff John Clark ran into my room and yelled at me to get up, that a big lot of men were mobbing the jail. The cause of this mob was that a lot of men had been apprehended with a whole herd of cattle that did not belong to them, and were put in jail.

James Trainer and myself went with Sheriff Clark to the jail and when we got within twenty steps of the mob, who were assembled at the jail door, we were ordered to halt, and that in tones that meant business. They told the Sheriff that they would not hurt us, provided we kept our distance. We backed off to the courthouse, say thirty steps from the jail and the Sheriff ran upstairs to a south room, put his rifle through the window and told the mob that the first damned man that touched that jail door, he would kill him. Seeing that they might have to kill all three of us, about ten men came right in by Trainer and myself, didn't even say "good evening" and went upstairs to talk to Clark. They told the Sheriff that they meant no harm to him or the county, but they were going to have those men, even if they had to hurt him in doing so. There were about forty men of the mob, Clark saw he was up against it. The Sheriff came down and told Trainer and myself to get off a little distance and watch them until he could go for help. While he was gone, the mob secured battering rams, broke the jail door, took five cattle rustlers out of the jail and started south with them.

When the Sheriff returned with five or six men, we started after them, all on foot except the Sheriff. We took a turkey trot down the Fredericksburg road about half a mile, when the mob began to shoot. We, thinking they were shooting at us, returned the fire, at the blaze of their guns, but got no answer. They had heard us coming, and were not through with their work, and commenced to shoot the men they had not hanged. The Sheriff being horseback, ran down to where the shooting was and found the two Baccus brothers and a man named Turley hanging to the limb of a tree, Wiggins with his brains shot out, and the fifth man gone. Sheriff Clark quickly cut the men down from the tree, and when I got there, I examined Turley, found his neck was not broken, and that he was still warm. I ran to a branch nearby, dipped water in my hat, ran back to Turley, poured it on him, rubbed him, and he soon showed signs of returning to life. He gradually came to life, with a glassy stare in his eyes. He could not talk until next morning. The Baccus brothers were both dead. The fifth man, Johnson, when we began to fire on them, jerked the rope over his head, jumped over the fence and went "on 21" across the plowed ground. Johnson was a tenderfoot and was only hired to drive the wagon and cook for the Baccus outfit. I think it was the third day after that, Johnson came to my camp, footsore and wild.

District court opened in Mason, and Judge Everett sent a messenger to me with a note saying "Don't turn Johnson over to any Sheriff or anyone. I will notify you when to have him here." The Judge sent out for Johnson, and we took him to Mason, under a safe guard. The Judge sent him before the grand jury, to see if he would identify any of the mob. Johnson could tell nothing of a positive nature and feigned to not know them. He was not prompted by anyone to tell, or not tell anything. But we were glad he did not tell any more than he did, as it might frustrate our plans of catching them. Also, we didn't know it but some members of that grand jury belonged to the mob. I was summoned before the grand jury, and they fired into me, and crossfired, until I began to think they were prying into state secrets. I knew nothing, at the time, that I thought the grand jury ought to have, and I parried them with the semi-truth, and we made a drawn battle.

In quick sequence, a man named William Coke was missing. Mr. Coke was foreman of a cattle ranch near Mason. The last heard of him, a man named Miller, who lived in Mason, had seen him on the range and talked with him. The Major ordered me to take a scout in search of Coke, and take Miller with me. Mr. Miller showed where he had seen Coke and talked with him, but no tracks could be found. A little later, one evening when old Sol had bade us all adieu in the west, Johnson went to Mr. Miller's residence in Mason and shot him. Johnson, thinking he had done him in, was never seen in that section again. Miller recovered. William Coke was never heard of, and we think his bones were bleaching in some cavern, so often the receptacle of crime.

Following in succession, when Daniel Hoerster, a prominent man, was riding down the street in Mason, he was shot off his horse and killed. The killing party started out of town, in a pretty lively gait, and Peter Jordan leveled down on them with a rifle, at long range. His bullet struck George Gladden's gun, just where his hand was grasping it, and tore Gladden's hand up badly, and almost demolished the breech of his gun. They escaped without further casualties.

By this time the feud was denominated Germans against Americans. This was not true. A short time after the killing at Mason, Sheriff Clark got into his buggy and drove down to Kellar's store, about 12 miles south of Mason, on the Llano River. Everybody there was on the watch. They saw two men coming up to the store, and when they got pretty close to the store, Sheriff Clark saw that they were Mose Beard and George Gladden. Those two men were considered among the fighting men opposing the Sheriff. They rode up and dismounted, and the Sheriff stepped out on the porch, with his rifle in hand, and the firing commenced at about 30 paces. Young Kellar was supporting Clark. John Clark was one of the blue hen's chickens. Within perhaps two minutes the firing ceased on

Beard and Gladden's side. Clark saw what was the matter. They were both mortally wounded. They could, however, get on a horse, and both mounted one horse. Gladden holding Beard on the horse, they rode back the way they came. The Sheriff got into his buggy and drove after them, taking Kellar and another man with him.

Within a mile and a half, they came upon them, on the bank of Beaver Creek. Beard was dying, and Gladden could go no further. Beard died within a short time after the officers got to him. Gladden was shot nine times. The Sheriff returned and sent his Deputy, James A. Baird, to take care of them. Mr. Baird found them, late in the night. He built up a big fire near the lifeless body of Mose Beard and was just starting for the nearest ranch to get a wagon to move Gladden, when he heard the mail hack coming. He waited for the hack and sent Gladden to his home in Loyal Valley on board the hack. Gladden got well. Kellar's store was their Waterloo on a fighting basis. The killing that followed was sneaking murder.

Some time afterward, Gladden killed Peter Barder, in Llano County, and was sent to the penitentiary for 99 years. Mr. Barder was considered a killer on the other side of the feud. Gladden was pardoned, after serving some time in the penitentiary. About the first of all this killing, John Worley was brutally murdered by Scott Cooley, on suspicion that he had helped to kill Williamson.

The above constitutes the principal killing, in that horrible affair.

A casual observer may notice that no arrests were made on either side. However, we recall, that John Ringo, and a few others on the side opposing the civil authority were arrested and put in the Burnet County jail, but they made their escape without trial. The reason that no arrests were made can only rest upon hypothesis, and that is: the men supporting civil authority needed no arrest, and those opposing it urged equal claims of being right, but would not submit their grievances to law.

The Rangers could only support the civil authority in cases of actual bloodshed, as Mason County was not under martial law. The Rangers could arrest criminals indicted by the courts, and even more, they could arrest on information, or actual observance of crime, but Mason County had never brought a man to trial during this feud. Sheriff Clark, seeing that it would take eternal vigilance for him to live in Mason County, resigned the office of sheriff, and left for parts best known to himself. Other principal actors against him went to Arizona, then considered a far off land from Texas. The war died out and Mason County is now prosperous and happy.

Rio Grande Campaign

In 1878, I resigned the command of Company D and went to Houston, Texas. Lieutenant Frank Moore was put in command of the Company, and the Company was stationed on the headwaters of the Llano River, until a little unpleasantness came up on the Mexican border. The nature of that trouble was that some Mexicans, from the Mexican side, came over to the Texas side, and committed some offenses that caused their arrest and they were tried by the County Judge at Rio Grande City and penalties assessed against them, to cause their imprisonment. This incensed the Mexicans to a high pitch, and they came over from the Mexican side and liberated the Mexican prisoners, and in the row shot the County Judge. But the wound was not serious. This raised Cain on the border and Companies A and D of the Rangers were ordered there immediately.

Major Jones wrote to me in Houston, that if I would come back and take command of my old company, that he would insure me a captaincy, and that pay would be better, etc. I concluded to do it, came to Austin, received a captain's commission signed by Governor O. M. Roberts, proceeded to Laredo, where my old company was stationed, and took command of the Company.

Captain Neal Coldwell, who was Captain of Company A had the command of Company D until I arrived. He had camped both companies near old Fort McIntosh, which was garrisoned by the United States soldiers. We talked to Captain Coldwell as to what his opinion was regarding the situation, and his keen observance led me to believe that there would be no fight with Mexico.

Pardon a little yarn.—Two negro boys were discussing the rank of army officers, as they walked down the street, according to their shoulder straps and epaulets, and noticing an orderly sergeant, who had more stripes than any of them, one boy said to the other "Dat's mor 'n any Cap'n!" So it was with Captain Coldwell. He was more than any captain in ability, and one of the best officers in the service. We worked with him or rather under his orders, until we could learn what he knew regarding the situation on the Rio Grande. By his suggestion, we moved both companies down the Rio Grande. I stopped my company at Carrizo, just opposite the town of Guerrero, in Mexico. Captain Coldwell took station at Ringgold barracks, some sixty miles below me. We had sort of a grapevine line to headquarters at Austin, by courier from his camp to mine, thence to Laredo, where we could reach the wires.

After I had been at Carrizo a short time I ventured to go over to the town of Guerrero, in Mexico. Guerrero was twelve miles from the river where I crossed at Carrizo. I went alone and the public road had no charms for me, and I took to the chaparral and rode into Guerrero. Just as I entered the town, I rode into a nest of loafers and a few soldiers with them, and the scoundrels knew me. They cursed me for everything vile, and I pretended not to understand them, but I understood every word they said. I played the baby act successfully and rode on into the town. I strolled around like an innocent spectator and finally I came upon a Mexican merchant, who was a nice and intelligent man. Then I had found a man that I wanted to talk to. He thought that there would be no immediate danger of any eminent trouble between the two countries and assured me that the more intelligent class of Mexican citizens were decidedly friendly to us. I could see no heavy war clouds around Guerrero, and took to the brush like a wild turkey, back to the ferry at Carrizo. Then I was under cover of my own guns and the boys were watching for me at the bank of the river.

In a day or two later, I thought I would move camp down to Roma, about forty miles below Carrizo, and on the morning that I took up march for Roma, the Mexican soldiers from Guerrero started for Mier, opposite Roma, and made the distance in one day on foot. They were on the *qui dad* as well as I was. When I had been at Roma a few days and learned the cow trails and crossings of the river, I went over to Mier. It was an opportune time, as a big fiesta was going on there and the presence of strangers was expected. Mier was 15 miles from Roma.

The features of the fair were bull fighting and gambling. The Mexican women would walk up to a gambling table, place large sums of money on a card, and win or lose, and you would not hear a word from them. Everything was perfect order in the gambling place. The women smoked cigarettes and yet they appeared to be perfect ladies. I though it was the most wonderful thing that I had ever seen, that gambling could be tolerated to an apparent point of decency. We learned another feature in their realm of society: when a girl or woman nurses a child of doubtful parentage, it is not considered a disgrace, but a misfortune. I have often thought of that, that they could wear the mantle of charity with more comfort than our own people. Their ideals are as widely apart from ours as the poles, consequently I don't think we can ever assimilate in one idea of government. Altogether, the fiesta was unique and interesting.

Ostensibly, we were there attending the feast, but our wicked eyes were on other matters as well. We surveyed the soldiery, and their equipments. Also we were watching for criminals, whose description we had. We took time to view the historic old spot of Mier, where the Santa Fe prisoners drew white and black beans, in their lottery for life. There stands out the most noble thing in American history, where one man who had drawn a white bean giving him his liberty, offered to swap it to his comrade for a black one that he had drawn, which condemned him to death. The man with the black bean was just as brave and noble and refused to take the white bean.

We returned to Roma, looked after some little matters in helping the customs guards, or river guards, as they were called, and considered the outlook in general. After having been at Roma about two months we concluded that the war scare was a chinook wind, and had gotten back to normal temperature. Being under sort of *carte blanche* orders, we moved the company back to Laredo.

At Laredo, we found the old conditions of bandit trouble still rampant, and white men and Mexicans plying their trade, on both sides of the river. We were not diplomats, and were not sent there for that purpose, but we formed a sort of a junta with the Mexican Major, who was commanding the Mexican soldiers at New Laredo. We interpreted our junta into international law, but we fear it would not have looked much like it at Washington City. I was afraid of our good old Governor Roberts, for he was certainly a straight edge but, if our doings had been reported to Major Jones, we think he would have turned his head in a different direction. I think I had some the best of the Mexican Major in our treaty.

The Mexican government had what they called a *zona libre* (free belt) extending back one mile into Mexico, from the Rio

Grande River. This may have been regarding customs duties, but we interpreted it to mean "catch them if you can, in one mile of the river." The Mexican Major was a shrewd man, and a gentleman, and although we had not met each other many times, our work was done through agencies. I may be telling too much, but if Uncle Sam wants to try me at this late date, prison life would not cheat me out of many years. He would find no documentary evidence, and not many witnesses living. If the Mexican Major is living, we think his government should give him a pension.

Now, I will tell you of some of our crimes. The Mexican Major made a scout down the river, on his side and found one of the most noted bandits that infested that country, and in a running fight with him, several miles before he reached the river, failed to get him, but as he was swimming the river he shot him, wounding him badly, but he reached the Texas side, in close proximity to his bandit quarters. The Major sent a messenger to me immediately, telling me where he had crossed the river and that he had probably reached the den of bandits on our side. We sent a scout immediately down the river, and in the settlement, or ranch, where the Major said he crossed, my men found him, badly wounded, but brought him up to Laredo and put him in jail. There was an arrest made by the Rangers, without a warrant for arrest and on information from the Republic of Mexico. But we knew the evidence could and would be brought against him to convict him on our side, and if he was not extradited we would fix him in Texas.

Shortly after that, a Mexican was coming into New Laredo from the interior of Mexico, with some fancy goods to sell at New Laredo, including some very fine Mexican hats. He was held up about twenty miles from Laredo, and robbed of everything he had by Mexicans. He came into Laredo and reported it to the Major in command, and he sent the man right over to me. The Major advised me to send a scout up the river, and he would send a scout up the river on his side. I sent a scout up the river, and about 25 miles above Laredo they came in sight of an old ranch located on the river. When they got near the ranch they saw some men running away from the ranch, and making for the river. The Rangers ran up to the ranch, looked in the old building and saw some fine Mexican hats and other goods in there, which told them that those men were the robbers.

The Rangers put spurs to their horses and made the gravel fly in pursuit. They got to the river just as the robbers were getting out of the water on Mexican soil. That water didn't stop the Rangers much. They were onto their job. Very soon the bullets began to fly at the robbers, and they ran into a chaparral thicket and the Rangers kept fogging them, until they all quit their horses and took cover through the thick brush. Just then the Mexican scout came up from the Mexican side. They had heard the firing of the Rangers' guns, but were not alarmed about any war in Mexico, as they knew what it meant. The Rangers and Mexican soldiers all came back across to the old ranch, and the Rangers were armed of course. They rested there together and had a jolly time. The Rangers turned over the horses that they had captured in Mexico to the Mexican soldiers, and brought the old Mexican peddler's goods back to Laredo. He was notified that we had his goods, and came over and got them. I don't know whether he paid any duty on them or not.

There stood Fort McIntosh bristling with dress parade, bowed up like a mad bull, waiting for the enemy to make a lunge at her. But, the officers of the garrison were not to be blamed, as they were only machine guns. A few other like incidents made the bandits hard to catch up and down that river, many miles from Laredo. The businessmen and citizens threw their hats in the air over our success. We were willing to give the Mexican Major more than half the credit, as we could have done but little without his help. Thinking our treaty with Mexico will only be taken as a joke, we give the people of that border the benefit of the joke. The merchants and business-men, together with a large majority of the citizens wrote and signed a petition to Governor Roberts to keep us at Laredo. Also, gave me a copy of the petition which I have yet. But, there was an intervening order, which none of us knew of, which reached us at Laredo, ordering us back to the north-ern frontier of Texas. So their petition was not acted upon by the Governor. Captain Coldwell, who was stationed at Rio Grande City, about 100 miles below Laredo, also received marching orders, and brought his company up to Laredo, and we took up march together back to our old stamping ground on the northern border.

I will not get out of sight of Laredo without telling you something of banking there. Mr. E. J. Hall did the principal banking at Laredo. Mr. Hall invited us to inspect his bank and pass on its unique features. We were not a committee, or any part of one, to look after state or national banks, but Hall wanted us to enjoy the funny part of it. Mr. Hall had stacks of silver that looked like cord wood, in his counting room, and at his pay desk. This was mostly Mexican dollars and was hauled there by mule teams. When Texas livestock buy-ers visited the neighborhood of Laredo to purchase Mexican stock, they had only to go to Ed Hall's bank, and see how his stock of money was holding out. They didn't have to inquire about securities and the men selling livestock did their own inspecting. It was all in sight, and no watered collaterals behind it. The dark and gruesome spectre of panics did not bother Mr. Hall. He knew Wall Street, and few men knew it better. We took a toddy with Mr. Hall, and wished him a long and prosperous career in Rio Grande banking. If there is any moral in this, it points to a sound money basis. He had a gold reserve to meet any requirement of gold legislation, but the endless chain that Grover Cleveland had to contend with was left to the stalwarts of financial juggling.

On the March

We left Laredo under secret orders to move Company D to Uvalde County, and to await further orders. Guessing was in order, and my men discussed the matter around the campfire; and the topic lasted for months. They knew nearly as much about it as I did, and developments were slow. I kept my guess to myself, which was, that we would not be moved too far from the Rio Grande until the low rumblings of discontent died out with Mexico. Captain Pat Dolan had worked Uvalde County pretty well along the line of local disorders, and we could afford to go fishing.

We camped Company D twelve miles east of Uvalde, on the Sabinal River, and on the mail line from San Antonio to Uvalde. Captain Coldwell's Company A moved on up to the headwaters of Guadalupe River, under command of First Sergeant George Arrington. (Mr. Arrington was subsequently commissioned a captain in the Frontier Battalion.) We were somewhat restless in our Sabinal camp. Our training had been, "under quick orders and fight for results." There were only a few petty artists in that neighborhood, whose occupation ran down as low as stealing a pair of hobbles, and we waited on them just to keep our hands in. We went sure enough fishing, to the Frio River, eight miles from camp. Mrs. Roberts went with us, in the ambulance, together with three Rangers. In breaking through thick brush to get to a large water hole we knew of we spied a real leopard, which seemed to be surveying us as undesirable citizens. He appeared to be tame, but we didn't try to pet him. We let him go "Scott free."

When we reached the water and cast our lines, we looked down the river to a shoal and could see an object that looked unusual, as we knew that spot quite well, from frequent visits there to a wild turkey roost. We laid aside our fish poles, and went to investigate. When we got to the object we saw that it was a dead man floating on top of the water. We sent Mrs. Roberts back to camp, and to get help to take care of him. Sergeant L. P. Sieker returned with three or four men, and took him out of the water, when he found a very large rock tied to his middle, which we weighed subsequently, thinking we might need it in the possibility of future evidence. The rock weighed 52 pounds.

We stayed there to try our hand as detectives. We surveyed the appearance of things in sight, and concluded that the man had been thrown off of a big bluff, on the west side of the river, and that the rock held him at or near the bottom, until he floated to shallow water and came to the surface. He was so bleached by the water that we couldn't tell whether he was a white man or a Mexican. We climbed up the bluff, on the west side, and were working through the thick chaparral brush, when we came upon a horse track leading towards the bluff. There we could plainly see where the man was thrown off the bluff. We examined closely and could see where the man had brushed the dirt bank, in falling some twelve feet to the water.

In looking closely we saw a large butcher knife lodged in some little roots near the water. How I should get that knife without swimming confronted me with doubt. I could see some little twigs growing in the dirt bank and I thought I would risk holding to those, and if I went in, it would be the whole hog with my clothes on. I held on to those twigs with fear and trembling, until I reached the knife and threw

it on top of the bank. I crawled up again to footing and examined the knife. It had a wooden handle, and on the handle
some cattle brands were cut, the insignia of where the knife
belonged. I back-tracked the horse to a big road that led up
to Dillard's ranch, about two and a half miles from the river,
then I had brought mystery to a more reasonable conclu-
sion—that the ranch could tell something about it.

I sent Sergeant L. P. Sieker to the ranch with three men, and
told him to arrest every man on that ranch, and we would
see if the old maxim would work, that "murder will out." I
knew that Sergeant Sieker could pull them if any other man
could. He arrested every man that he could find on the ranch
and they looked phenomenally wild. Sieker told them what
he had found, and tracked it to their door and told them that
they better "fessup." He was using a writ of rouster, but it
worked all right.

Finally a Mexican stepped up and said, "I am the man that
killed him." Then his explanation followed. The man that
was killed was a Mexican. The man that had killed him had
bought some horses from him, which all proved to be stolen horses, and were taken from him. The Mexican that was
killed had brought another bunch of horses to sell him, but,
he was so mad over the first transaction that he took his gun
and shot him. The horses he brought the last time were there
for inspection. We looked them over and found a fine buggy
horse that belonged to Joe Rogers, who was a friend of mine,
and lived near Austin. We knew the horse as well as our own
saddle horses, and when we saw him we said, "Good shot."
But Sergeant Sieker took the Mexican and the Dillard boys up
to Uvalde, put the Mexican under bond to await the action
of the grand jury. We whispered to the boys, "Don't appear
against them," and that ended it.

We wintered in 1878, on Sabinal River, and when spring came we began to feel like loafers. But we were soon relieved of monotony. Matters on the northern border, and in our old district, were coming to life, on a basis of murder and pillage. So we got double quick orders to go back there. My boys felt like lazy school boys that enjoy a good recess. They whooped and yelled, and flew at the wagons and pack mules and we were soon on the march for the head of the San Saba River, some 250 miles from Sabinal.

Within a few days' march, we began to reach our volunteer reserve. My men could borrow a suit of clothes, a horse and saddle, or anything a ranch had. And in some tough little fights, you could hardly tell who were Rangers and who were not. But it was all for the State of Texas. We wore no uniform, except that of citizens and there was no making faces at each other, as between the citizens and uniformed soldiers. We struck camp four miles below Fort McKavett, on the San Saba River. And after regulating camp matters, securing supplies and forage, and the routine, I will soon hand you something from the frontier bulletin board. I may not give the dates correctly but, from first to last, these are our most important dates, covering our whole service.

FORT DAVIS SCOUT

About the 25th of June, 1880, I got a telegram from Judge Frazier, coming from Fort Stockton, Texas, asking for help. Stockton was 250 miles from our camp. The sense of this telegram was that five men had robbed the merchants and sacked the town of money and all valuables that they wanted and had gone on up to Fort Davis, repeating the same thing there. Fort Davis was garrisoned by several companies of U. S. soldiers. The citizens could get no help from them as they could only act as a *posse comitatus*. The Rangers issued a kind of a writ they called *Veni, Vidi, Vici*. I believe that means "I came, I saw, I conquered."

They arrested some of the county officials and put their own men to guard the jail. My only having detailed seven men to go with Sergeant Ed Sieker, who was in charge of the scout, made eight men in all, but Sergeant Caruthers, of the Ranger force, had come as fast as the mail hack could bring him, from the City of Austin, and joined my men at Fort Davis, making nine all told. The robbers were the last of the Billy the Kid bunch that had operated in New Mexico. Their names were Jesse Evans, John Gunter and three of the Davis brothers. But they had so many aliases that identity by name was impossible, but they passed by these names in New Mexico.

They had left Fort Davis a day or two before my men got there and the Rangers found out that they went west. Sergeant Sieker divided his men at Davis, leaving private Miller, E. J. Pound, Nick Brown and Henry Thomas to guard the jail. Sergeant Ed Sieker took five men with him, who were R. R.

Russell, D. T. Carson, S. A. Henry, Sergeant Caruthers and George Bingham, also a Mexican guide. They left Fort Davis at 9 p.m. and at 1 p.m. the next day came in sight of the robbers. They were about a mile ahead of the Rangers and, the boys being eager to get to them, struck a little faster gait, which move caused the robbers to leave the road they were on and strike for a canon some distance from the road. The Rangers seeing that, started straight for them at good speed. The bandits reached the gulch first and dismounted and took shelter behind big rocks which fringed the break of the gulch. Sergeant Sieker, R. R. Russell, D. T. Carson and George R. Bingham were the only ones riding Ranger horses and the others could not keep up. So the fight fell on Sieker, Carson, Russell and Bingham.

As the Rangers approached, firing commenced from behind those rocks, two bullets striking Carson's horse and one through the brim of his hat, and Bingham was shot dead. Carson, Sieker and Russell dismounted, and as George Davis showed up from behind a rock to shoot, Sergeant Sieker and Carson fired at him almost simultaneously. Sieker's bullet struck him in the breast and, as he fell, Carson's bullet went through his head. The other bandits, seeing the quick work of the Rangers, knew some more of them had to go, and they broke and ran under the bluff, out of sight from the Rangers and got under some shelving rocks.

The Rangers were hunting them like blood hounds and one of them yelled out that they would surrender, if they, the Rangers, would not hurt them. Sergeant Sieker told them to come out. They came out, gave up their arms, and were taken back to where the firing commenced, and just then the Mexican guide came up and told them that one of their men was killed. They had not missed poor Bingham, who was lying dead, not over seventy-five yards from them. He, being behind when they ran up into the fight, had received a dead shot. The Rangers were so furious over losing one of their comrades, that cartridges began to fly into their guns almost automatically, to finish them up, while the poor devils were begging for life. R. R. Russell was the first man to throw a cartridge into his gun barrel, and the first man to say "Don't kill them."

Mr. Russell is now President of the State Bank and Trust Company, in San Antonio, Texas, and is reputed to be worth nearly two million dollars. Dick Russell doesn't think that he was any better than Bingham, Sergeant Sieker or D. T. Carson, who are all dead, but remembers them with that fellow feeling and friendship that characterizes God's most noble men.

This fight occurred on the 3rd day of July, 1880. They buried the dead on July 4th, on the road from Fort Davis to Paso Del Norte, 18 miles from the Rio Grande. The citizens of Fort Davis gave the Rangers, on their return to jail with those prisoners, $500 in cash and the citizens of Fort Stockton gave them $600 in cash. The Rangers didn't consider that a pay job, but received the money thankfully. The citizens appeared to think that nothing was too good for those poor tired and hungry boys that had put in night and day on that long scout to protect them.

On return of the Rangers to Fort Davis they arrested John Selman, who was jailer there. Selman was the man who killed John Wesley Hardin, some years later. So you can see that County Judge Frazier and the Rangers wrought a mighty change there in a short time.

The prisoners were not allowed bond and were kept in jail at Fort Davis until district court set. The grand jury found bills against them. By this time the Davis brothers had to disclose their true identity, as they had to have help. Their parents lived in Texas and were highly respected and wealthy. But, for their sake, we withhold their right names from further publicity. We let them go to trial under their robber aliases. John Gunter and Jesse Evans were tried under those names and received long terms in the penitentiary. The Davis brothers managed to get bonds, by putting off trial and the bonds were forfeited and paid, and that ended their trial. The trial judge is dead and gone and we will say nothing more about it. The men that were in that scout are all dead, except R. R. Russell, who lives in San Antonio; S. A. Henry, who lives on Nueces River in Edwards County, and Sergeant Caruthers, near Alpine, in Brewster County. Those three should have a reunion, in memory of the silent dead that served on that scout. They broke up the most noted band of outlaws that ever infested any state or country.

THE POTTER SCOUT, 1880

I had not been in camp many days, when a messenger arrived from 30 or 40 miles west, who had come through torrents of rain, to inform me that his ranch and neighbors had lost a number of horses, and he was satisfied that white men had stolen them. This messenger was Sam Merk, and he came of his own volition. Sam was one of my standbys, to help me. I detailed a scout to go back with Merk to find the trail, which I knew would be difficult on account of the rain having put it out. The detail numbered seven men, as follows: Sergeant R. G. Kimble, in charge of scout, N. J. Brown, Ed Dozier, William Dunman, J. V. Latham, R. C. Roberts and M. Smith.

When the scout was ready to move, I told them to "catch them if they stayed on top of the ground." This was not exactly an order, but rather bad advice, as I had not considered state lines. It dawned upon me a little later that we were state troops. I was a little skittish on that score, just having been rounded up pretty hard by our good old Governor Roberts, for an incident that occurred, involving international law.

I will tell it, before resuming the scout. Sergeant J. B. Gillett, was on detached service on the Rio Grande and at El Paso. He was notified by the civil authorities at Socorro, New Mexico, that a certain Mexican, giving his name and description, had killed an editor at Socorro and fled to Mexico. Gillett incidentally took a little *paseo* into Mexico and, finding the man, lured him to American soil. On this side, Gillett nailed him and wired Socorro that he would be up with him, on a certain train. The train was held up by a mob within a mile of Socorro, the man taken from Gillett, and hanged to a cottonwood tree. The Mexican consul at Washington, pounced upon Governor Roberts for a genuine case of kidnapping. Our Governor replied that if Sergeant Gillett did that, he was responsible for it, as it was by no authority of the state. While I had nothing to do with it, the Old Alcalde (Governor Roberts) took me to task. He gave me the name and address of every extradition officer on the Rio Grande and in sentences, that savored of whole spice, he told me to "not let such a thing as that occur again." I took it like a little boy that had been stealing watermelons, and was glad to get off that way. Gillett didn't belong to my Company at that time.

Now, we resume the scout. The scout could get no trail of them, where the stock was taken, but guessing the course they would take, the scout bore a little north of west, in the direction of old Fort Lancaster on Live Oak Creek, near its junction with the Pecos River. When the scout reached Fort Lancaster, they heard of the men, passing there with the horses. But they rode two or three days behind them.

The scout pushed on up the Pecos several days, staying on their trail. Most of their horses were beginning to fail and Sergeant Kimble left five of the men near Horsehead Crossing on the Pecos and took William Dunman with him and followed on. About 150 miles up the Pecos they came to the Hashknife ranch, finding Billy Smith there in charge, he giving them information that the men had passed there with the horses. Finding they had gained on them pretty well, the Rangers felt encouraged but their horses were done up. Billy Smith rounded up three of the best horses on the ranch, and went with them in pursuit. After traveling up the river a long distance, they noticed that the trail had quit the road. Thinking they had passed them, they turned back down the road to pick up the trail. They hadn't traveled far, when they saw the thieves coming to meet them. Sergeant Kimble thought that the parties would know him, and he quickly planned the attack.

He was right, as they proved to be Jim and John Potter, who both knew Kimble well. Kimble told Dunman and Billy Smith to slow up a little, and he would ride more brisk, so as to cover the space between them, as one of them was riding ahead of the horses and the other behind them, making about 50 yards between them. They could come down on them both at once. Kimble pulled his hat down a little over his face, and passed Jim Potter, and went on to John, and pulled down on him, demanding his surrender. At that moment firing commenced between Jim Potter, Dunman and Smith. John Potter pulled at the breech of his gun, which was in a scabbard to his saddle, and Kimble warned him to turn it loose or he would kill him. John jumped off his horse, still pulling at the gun, and Kimble shot him. Sergeant Kimble looked around, at the other end of the fight, when he saw Jim Potter down with three bullet holes in him, and Smith and Dunman's horses both shot.

Just then a strange coincidence came in: Frank Potter, a brother of Jim and John Potter, heard the firing and came to them, finding his brothers both shot down but not dead. It is a certain fact that the Potters knew nothing of the whereabouts of each other. Frank Potter was a very good man, and was working on a cattle ranch some miles away. Jim and John were removed to a ranch, some eight or ten miles away, and Frank helped to take care of them until Jim died, two days later, and the Rangers took John to Fort Davis for treatment, where he finally recovered. They brought John back to Kimble County, and I turned him over to the sheriff, and he took him to San Antonio jail, for safekeeping. When district court set in Kimble County, the sheriff, Joe Clemens, went after him. While returning with the prisoner, at the head of the Guadalupe River a mob overpowered Sheriff Clemens and shot Potter to death.

WAITING ON THE COURTS

O ur activity in putting down cattle theft, mail robbery, and all kinds of lawlessness, entailed upon
us nearly the whole duty of reestablishing civil
government in the frontier districts. Consequently, our appearance in the district courts, against criminals, became a
necessity. We waited on all courts, except the kangaroo vari-
ety and even instituted that in camp. We hardly knew whether
we were Rangers, or court officers. The number of arrests we
made could not be enumerated without our adjutant general's
reports. We gained the ill-will of all evil-doers and they were
our bitter enemies.

We began to think that we could tell, when we made an arrest, whether the man was guilty or not. If he belonged to the
Buckskin Joe class, he would begin to chant some little song,
of wild and woolly origin, which would tell the company he
had been in. If, on the other hand, he was shrewd and capable
of doing big mischief, he would deport himself nearly like
a gentleman, as the circumstances would admit of, but, his
linking himself up with legitimate business and responsible
men, was where he fell down.

The class of Texas criminals in those days was different to
what they are now. In those days, they had collected on the
frontier in numbers to defy the law and instituted plans that
would protect them from the law. Since the advent of the railroad we first got the "tramp", and we must say, that name is
an unfair epithet, applied to poor men, out of employment,
whether they are indigent or unfortunate. The professional

tramp is the spawn of crowded cities, bred under conditions that were foreign to American spirit, that simply made him a creature, hunting sustenance to satisfy hunger. Next came the professionals, burglars, cracksmen, robbers, and hold-ups of every description, that were runaways from municipal governments of large cities. Texas was not as good a field as they had supposed, owing to the vast territory the state covered and no big cities to shelter them from identity, as almost every man knows his neighbor, and strangers were spotted without difficulty. So, after getting rid of the original Texas outlaw, the Eastern aftermath has been handled with care with Pandora's box labeled *This Side Up*. While Texas is not entirely immune from evil or infractions of law, we believe she is the peer of any state, along the line of good government.

If the Rangers can claim a small part in this, it reverts back to the state which maintained that service. We can only claim a modest share as citizens. Our work may have some merit, in handling the Indian trouble, and we leave the citizens of the frontier and progress of the state to answer for us. I set out to record the services of Company D Frontier Battalion, but not to particularize our company as being most prominent. I was in possession of the correct data of my company's work, and have partially given it, in simple justice to the brave men that served with me. There were five other companies in the Frontier Battalion, and that each of them did good service is not left to criticism but to their several honorable records.

Company D survived my resignation from the service, and did splendid work along old lines, until it was minimized by niggardly appropriations, and could hardly maintain a corporal guard. The spirit was in the men, but the handicap ruled them down to such subordination that they lost the prestige of doing things in the Ranger way. They did fine service, as only a small auxiliary branch of the civil government, but lost the lead as a state force. The state was right in this, as the Ranger service had served the splendid purpose for which it was organized, at least to the extent that put the border counties safely in the hands of their civil officers. But the state showed her gratitude, in almost a pathetic way, by preserving the name Ranger, in allowing a small organization to exist under that name. This involves a fine point, allowing the Rangers to be a military organization, which cropped out in the present Mexico troubles. If they are only state troops, their work is preceding martial law. I take it that their work can only follow in the wake of civil authority, unless they are declared militia.

THEY WERE MODESTLY, AND INNOCENTLY, GREAT FROM BIRTH.

-CAPT. D. W. ROBERTS ON EARLY TEXANS

PEGLEG STAGE ROBBING, 1880

There was a stage station on the San Saba River, on the Fort Mason and Fort McKavett road, the distance being about 80 miles between Mason and McKavett, and Pegleg was just halfway between the two. A series of stage robbings had been kept up near Pegleg station for a long time, and the robbers had not been apprehended.

We detailed a man to go with the stagecoach while passing this notorious piece of road. He would lie down on top of the coach, with a double-barreled shotgun in his grip, to await developments. The stage driver didn't dare to make a fight with the robbers and the passengers were generally unarmed. No stage robbing occurred for a considerable time, and we concluded that the real robbers had been informed of what was going on. We recalled the Ranger from his lofty perch on the coach. But little time had passed when the stage was robbed again near Pegleg. This time there were several passengers on the coach, including an officer of the U. S. army. This officer was plucky, and tried to make a fight on them with a little .38 calibre pistol, which would only have served to get him killed. The other passengers had to take hold of him, to stop him, as they thought it would cause all of them to be killed.

Only two robbers appeared. The robbers went through the passengers, then cut open the mail sacks, and took all valuables to be found. The drivers thought it was not much use to sew up the mail sacks, as it was costing Uncle Sam too much to furnish them. The officer lost some money, his little shooter, and other things valuable to him. When the stage came up opposite my camp, this officer sent me a list, with description of the things taken from the passengers.

I thought it not much use to lose twenty miles riding to pick up a cold trail, and I took four men with me and started due east, to cut sign. After I had traveled six or eight miles, I saw four men riding straight across my course and going north. I thought I had them. I bore in slightly towards them. I saw them fixing their guns for business, but I made no demonstration to show them that I saw it. I got up in talking distance of them, and knew them, which confirmed it more with me that they were the right men. I jollied them a little, but kept gaining on them. I saw they had their guns across their saddles, in front of them. They were riding in a straight breast, with their thumbs on the hammers of their guns. I tried to engage them in "very pleasant conversation."

A man named Jackson was riding on the left of their breast, thumb on the hammer of his gun, and I knew he was a bad hombre. I rode up nearly to his side, but was careful to not get before the muzzle of his gun, and almost as quick as lightning, I jerked my pistol and shoved it against him, telling him to turn that gun loose or I would kill him. At the same instant, my men covered them from the rear. Jackson was stubborn, and held to his gun until he could almost feel my bullet, when his hands limbered and his courage likewise.

I made them dismount, and made them take their clothes off down to stockings, and examined them carefully for the articles missing from the stage passengers. They had some sacks tied to their saddles which were full of clothing, all new. I could find nothing that came off the stage. I fired off their guns, told them to dress, which they did, and in meantime, I was figuring what to do with them.

I knew I had arrested them without a warrant, and an idea struck me. I told them if they would leave that country, and never bother me or people living there again, I would turn them loose. This brightened them up, almost to a feeling of friendship and they promised me that they would leave for keeps. They did leave, and were not seen there any more. And the Pegleg stage was not robbed any more.

My theory was, (after I found out they had robbed a store, south of there, securing the goods I found in their sacks) that, they had failed to connect with the two that robbed the mail, but had to get away from there just the same. After we parted, we viewing their backs until they were out of gun shot, one of my boys began to laugh. He had found a name for me. He called me "Pecos Bob." Pecos Bob was a character that prided himself on drawing first and getting the drop on his victim. (Pecos Bob was Bob Ollinger). My men joked me pretty much as they pleased, for they had to, in self defense. My dignity as an officer only reached to positive orders, that were obeyed to a letter, and after that, my men and myself met on a common plane of friendship.

Along this line of work, Major Jones once made what we called a roundup in a locality where those fellows almost had their sway. And by a concerted move, which was done in one day, every man that could be found was brought to camp. The better people of that section didn't object to this, and the worse ones, being in the herd had little grounds for objections, as all fared alike. The Major with his keen sagacity and knowledge of them, enabled him to sort them out to the "Queen's taste." That move made economy in work, and alarmed the whole fraternity of evil-doers. They didn't know but that Colonel Roy Bean's law (the law west of the Pecos) had prevailed all over the state.

It was not exactly martial law, but a kind of writ of rouster. Company D was used for this job—the Company was then under the command of Lieutenant Frank Moore. The bad men didn't know what to look for next and began to strike for tall timber. The Pecos country, New Mexico and Arizona caught an unenviable lot of them.

By this time, we were getting the support of the best citizens, and their untiring help almost put them in the ranks of the Rangers. Our camp was their headquarters, and their homes were our welcome resting places. They furnished us anything that our temporary needs might call for, without any charge against the state and many a hungry Ranger shared their hospitality.

STEALING SADDLES

While we were encamped in Kimble County, my boys had become a little gay as society men, and attended the numerous dances given by the citizens, where they were welcome and received marked attention. On one occasion of a great *baile*, I gave permission to four of my men to attend the dance. I could hear expressions in camp of certain young ladies, being about the idea of the Rangers, as about all that was beautiful and proper, and in turn the young ladies had conferred upon them degrees of knighthood that would put the Arabians to flight.

This dance was given at Junction City, in Kimble County, eight miles south of my camp. Deputy Sheriff Joe Clemens made my camp his business headquarters, and on this occasion he went to the dance with my men. They tied their horses all together, leaving their saddles on the horses and left no guard with them. They brushed up their suits, and adjusted collars, and went to the ballroom as gay as larks. They realized their visions of pleasure, until just before daylight when they returned to their horses to come to camp. Lo and behold, two of the Rangers had lost their saddles, and Sheriff Clemens had lost his. It was fortunate they could get out of town before daylight, to cover the humiliation they felt. Sheriff Clemens came to camp with them, and of all the crestfallen boys they looked the worst.

Clemens was to break the news to me, which he did, and he shared fully the discomfort of the Rangers. I tried to look sour about it, but my amusement was too great. There were certain parties in the country there, whom I had put under my ban of suspicion, and they were constantly so, notwithstanding their galvanized appearance. I questioned Sheriff Clemens, as to whom he had seen in the town that night. He told me of the outsiders that he had noticed; of course they would not come into the ballroom, except to peep in, so as to locate the Rangers. I told Clemens to stay right there in camp that day and to make no demonstrations of search to create any excitement, and when night came to come with me and we would get the saddles. This statement seemed to astound him.

Mr. Clemens was a ranchman, as well as sheriff, and knew every cow trail in that vicinity. I knew that the parties who stole the saddles would leave a spy at Junction City, to see what would be done, and to inform the others if they were in danger. Just after dark, I took five men with me, including the two men that had lost their saddles, so that they could identify their saddles, also Sheriff Clemens went with me. We passed around the town of Junction City, so that no one would see us, and crossed the Llano River to the south and gained a high ridge, or divide, running west in the direction I wanted to go, to get to the camp of the parties I suspected, the distance being fifteen or twenty miles from Junction City. We reached one of the camps just before daylight, and went in on them in the innocent occupation of sleep. We found one of the men there that I had suspected. We invited him out to take breakfast with us, and the invitation was so pressing that he didn't resist it.

We took him about one and a half miles west, to where a road passed up Chalk Creek, running up to these camps from the Llano River, and from the main road that ran up the River. We stopped on the road to get breakfast and put out a picket above, and below us on the road, with orders to bring anyone to camp that might pass that way. Of course, this was simple hospitality, to give them breakfast, but it was not appetizing to some of them. One of the pickets brought Charles Beardsley up to breakfast. I knew Mr. Beardsley had been with Hensley, the first man captured, and his early mission was to give the news of what was going on at Junction City. I could get nothing out of Hensley regarding the saddles. After we had breakfast, I told three of my men to stay there at the campfire with Beardsley. I would take Hensley up into a little cedar brake, close by. After I was out of sight, they were to fire off their guns, turn Beardsley loose, and come on up to where I was, which was done according to orders.

Hensley heard the firing of the guns, and looked at me with a chilly sensation and said to me, "Captain, they have killed that man." I didn't answer him directly, but said to him, "Now if you know anything about those saddles, you had better tell it quick." I saw his lips began to quiver, and the tears began to trickle down his cheeks, when he said to me, "Captain, if you will let me go, and not punish me, I will show you the saddles." He was only eighteen or nineteen years old, and looked like he would be a better boy in different company. So I told him I would turn him loose if he showed up the saddles, provided that he would leave there, and quit the company he was in. He assured me that he would leave immediately, and go east to his home and stay there.

He took us to the saddles, which were hidden in a big shin-oak thicket, not far from where we found him, and the saddles looked like they could almost speak the praise of redemption. We put the saddles on the pack mule and went down into the public road that passed up the river from Junction. Sheriff Clemens was riding with me, and after some silence he said, "I'll be damned if this don't beat anything I ever saw." We had not gone far down the road, when we met the principal actor in the saddle stealing, who had stayed back, at Junction to listen for thunder. We wanted him anyway, and took him back with the saddles.

My boys that lost the saddles were very tender on the subject, and it would have been absolutely cruel to have teased them about it. Beardsley told subsequently that my men shot at him, and one of the men whose saddle was stolen sent him word that if he didn't stop that lying "he would wear him out with a quirt."

The man we brought back with the saddles was not tried for saddle stealing, but was sentenced to a two year term in the penitentiary for cattle stealing. He made his escape, with irons on him, and was not apprehended afterwards.

CATTLE STEALING

A few days after the saddle raid, a Mr. Evans, who lived in Mason County, reported to me that he had lost all his cattle, including his work oxen and in all had lost fifty-three head. He said the trail of the cattle had started west. I took a scout immediately and cut sign for the trail. I found the trail, going west, and followed it as rapidly as I could, but could not find anyone who had seen the parties or the cattle.

The trail went up the South Llano River for 25 miles, then bore south, to the head of the Frio River, that was called Frio Water Hole. After watering there, they struck straight west, to the head of the Nueces River. I was not far behind them at the Frio Water Hole. I could give a good guess then where they were taking the cattle. Fort Clark, near the Rio Grande was then a good market for butchers' cattle, and I was satisfied they were taking them there. We pushed on the trail, until about three o'clock in the evening when we reached the head of the Nueces River. The trail took down the old Fort Clark road, running down the river, and we were close to them. Within an hour's march, we were in sight of the dust caused by driving the cattle. The road ran through a dense growth of cedar, and shin-oak brush, and our chance to get the men was to catch them in some open space. We slowed up and watched for this chance, until they drove down into the bed of the river, where the road crossed, then we put spurs to our horses and ran in on them before they could cross, and captured them in the bed of the river. One of them tried to make a run, but we rounded him up before he got to the lead of the cattle.

There were only two men driving the cattle. One of them called himself Kiser; the other one we knew, and was satisfied that Kiser had gotten him into the stealing, as he was only 17 or 18 years old. I knew we could not get out of that brush that evening, with a lot of sore-footed and tired cattle, but drove back as far as we could, and camped for the night. Mr. Amon Billings happened to come by camp and said he could get us some feed for our horses before midnight, which he did. We hog-tied Señor Kiser with a rope and kept a guard over them that night, and managed to keep all our stock until daylight, after which, we soon reached the open country. We were four days getting back to camp with the cattle and prisoners. We notified Mr. Evans to come and get his cattle, and to say he was a proud man was barely expressing it, as it was about all the poor man had. Court was in session at Junction City, and Kiser was sent to the penitentiary for a long term, but escaped from the pen after serving only a short while.

Kiser took the trouble to tell me that he would kill me, if he had to follow to the end of the world. I paid no attention to his threat. Soon after this, I moved my camp back to the San Saba River. My own quarters were about 100 yards from the main Ranger camp, and facing it. One night, after my wife and myself had retired, someone rode up to the back of my tent, and hailed two or three times. I whispered to my wife to keep still. I reached for my gun, which I always had in reach, and quietly stepped out of the tent and walked around it, rather opposite from the open way, with my gun ready to fire. The visitor whirled his horse and ran off, muttering some low cuss words as he went. He must have seen the muzzle of my gun coming, in advance of his intended victim. I tracked him next morning, to where he went into the Fort McKavett road and from his horse tracks he had lost no time. There was a big bright guard fire in the Ranger camp, and I knew if it was anyone on square business, they would have gone to the guard first. I have always felt certain it was Kiser, but his nerve was not as good as he thought it was.

THE REAL RANGER HAS BEEN A VERY QUIET, DELIBERATE, GENTLE
PERSON WHO COULD GAZE CALMLY INTO THE EYE OF A MURDERER,
DIVINE HIS THOUGHTS, AND ANTICIPATE HIS ACTIONS, A MAN WHO
COULD RIDE STRAIGHT UP TO DEATH.

-WALTER PRESCOTT WEBB, *THE TEXAS RANGERS*

MAVERICKS

In the early days of Texas, say from 1845 to 1860, the cattlemen worked together, in perfect harmony, and to each other's interest. Mr. Sam Maverick was probably the largest cattle owner in the state at that time. So large was the area of his cattle range that he could hardly get over it in one season to mark and brand his calves. Mr. Maverick was a wealthy and influential man, and the small cattle owners looked out for his interest, together with their own.

Texas had enacted a law, that any animal, of the bovine kind, was public property after it became one year old and was not marked or branded, and was not following its mother. This was a bad law, but it was the law just the same. When the cattlemen were working their respective ranges and came upon a yearling that was not marked or branded, they generally conceded it belonged to Mr. Maverick. So common was the expression, Maverick, that they applied it straight to the animal, hence, an unmarked animal was a Maverick. The term Maverick became so common over the state that it was indeed general.

The stockmen tried to stay by the law, but so many men that had become handy with the rope, saw their advantage, and would take a yearling from its mother, although it might be sucking her, and call it a Maverick. Such men had but little invested in cattle, but would mark out a brand in the road if they had no paper to mark it on, and push cattle operations to an extent that would soon show that they were in it. Then, the fault of the law became glaring, and the Texas Legislators had to substitute criminal clauses in lieu of their slipshod liberality in the first law, allowing a yearling to be public property, provided it was not marked or branded.

Mr. W. J. Bryan's great expression, coined by himself, a "twilight zone" had not come into verbal use in those days but it was certainly in practical use by cattle rustlers to cover their deeds by law, anent open stealing. But broad open daylight stealing was the sequel of the mooted controversy. The legitimate cattle owners were the sufferers. In 1861, when the war between the states had become a bloody battle that called for all able-bodied men to enter the service, the State of Texas was literally covered with cattle, and their owners being called away, cattle were left to roam where they might and without attention. Those of the ranchmen that returned home after the war found their cattle scattered to the four winds and hundreds of them were three and four years old, without a mark or brand. This was particularly the case on the frontier of Texas. The rightful owners could not identify this unmarked stock, and they became public property again.

This situation invited every man that could get a few ponies and ropes, to enter the field, as though he was really a cattle owner, and according to his energy in the work, he succeeded in branding a very good herd in a short time. There was no market for cattle in Texas, and I have known parties to corral big numbers of cattle and kill them for the hides. A plug of tobacco was a standard price for a good yearling.

Kansas soon opened up as a cattle market, and driving herds to Kansas started up the cattle business again. John Chisum opened up the Chisum Trail to Kansas, over which many herds were driven. The cattle industry was then in the lead of cotton, and about the only source to get money to repair war losses. The man who could have reaped the greatest benefit out of cattle, by rightful ownership, could only hold their original branded stock, (and hardly that) on account of the conditions that had grown up beyond their control. Many large farmers, who had depended on negro labor, found themselves without an occupation, and some of them went into the cattle business. Such men generally made good, but they were up against the system of handling cattle, which, in many cases, amounted to open stealing.

Such conditions had enticed many men to come out on the frontier, who didn't own cattle, but could manipulate cattle rustlers to great advantage. They soon organized juntas that defied civil law, and the matter grew from bad to worse, until the armed power of the state had to be employed to stop it. The civil officers of the sparsely settled counties, could not handle them. This put the Rangers after the rustlers, which took a big part of their time, outside of fighting Indians and other enemies to the cattlemen. The cow men responded to our efforts like warriors and often faced the bullets with us, against the common enemy.

Thus, you will see, that after a cattleman had earned what he had, he had to fight to keep it. But, the power of the state, combining the splendid individual effort of the cattlemen, sustained the industry, and it still ranks as one of the greatest industries in the State of Texas. When cotton fails as a money crop, cattle stands between the people and the black Ghost of Panic, and sustains Texas, as one of the greatest states of the Union. I know but little of the methods of the Stockraisers' Association, but I do know that organized effort is the winning card in modern business ventures. I remember the first effort of the farmers, who organized what they called a Grange, which was later merged into the famous Alliance.

That was to protect the farmer from an undue tax, levied on them, by commercialism and the wily middleman who stood between the producer and his market, as a sinecure that neither produced or consumed, more than to keep individual selfishness alive. So it is with the stockraiser. He cannot afford to be at the mercy of organized capital, which is simply waiting to dictate to him what per cent he shall get out of his toil.

THE KILLING OF SAM BASS

Major John B. Jones had been making a trap for Sam Bass and his band for several years, and when the trap was finished and the triggers set, it proved to be a dead fall. Sam Bass was from Indiana and came to Texas and made his headquarters in Denton County and in the town of Denton, Texas. He was said to be a man of pleasant address and closely counterfeited a gentleman. He studied men and their character more than business and soon found a few that would work well in his cabinet. He, however, didn't believe distributing his patronage to many, as a grave trust, in his line, demanded men of steel nerve. He enlisted Jackson, one named Underwood and a man named Murphy, also Seba Barnes. This collection made by Bass was not done in one day, or in one year, but by long and careful study of those men, by passing on them, as competent for his service.

Bass was not a petty thief, but a bold robber. His biggest operations were not in Texas. He and his gang robbed a train in Nebraska and got $20,000 in gold. Bass and his men struck south, through the unsettled portion of Western Kansas and into the Panhandle of Texas, and continued down into Denton County. I don't suppose they saw a living white man in that thousand miles of travel. There was a thousand miles between them and any civil officer or detective, to ferret them out. The newspaper account of the robbery, the number that did it and the direction they started was all that could be found out. None of them were known where it happened. Bass and his party traveled by compass and came nearly straight to Denton.

By this time Major Jones had positive evidence of Bass' headquarters and his operations. The Major put some Rangers on the watch, not to positively invade the town of Denton, but to skirt around and find out what they could about Bass and his men, and to keep close under cover, regarding their identity as Rangers.

Captain June Peak was put there as the main worker on that job. I am not positive as to how it was accomplished, but Murphy had become known as one of the Bass gang and was approached in person or by letter, to see if he could be handled in the capture of the band. Major Jones was at Austin, conferring with the Governor, to see if he could offer Murphy immunity, if Murphy would work true in the matter.

The Governor, O. M. Roberts, agreed to free Murphy, if he would keep positive faith with Major Jones in capturing them. Murphy agreed to all the plans and corresponded with Major Jones as to where their next raid would be made, when they would all be together. The robbers planned to go to Round Rock, Texas, as they had learned that one of the merchants at Round Rock had a big lot of gold in his safe. This merchant was P. G. Peters, who now lives in New Mexico, and the same old safe is right here now in P. G. Peters' store. We have opened it many a time and always thought of Sam Bass.

The Major stayed at headquarters in Austin waiting to hear from Murphy again. The band met and started for Round Rock. When they got to Belton, in Bell County, which was about 50 miles from Round Rock, Murphy stepped into the post office and mailed a letter to Major Jones. This came near ending his life, as Bass had seen him enter the post office. When they went out of Belton, Bass put the matter straight to the band and they would have killed Murphy, only for the intervention of Jackson, who told them that they would have to kill him first. Murphy pleaded like a lawyer, stating that he had only stepped into the office to mail a letter to his people, as that might be the last one he would ever write. Although Murphy pleaded his own case, he didn't have a fool for his client. That was all that saved him. Murphy had stated in that letter when they would reach Round Rock. The Major had called in such Rangers as he wanted and had them in readiness to proceed to Round Rock, and upon receipt of Murphy's letter took them to Round Rock on double quick. The Major ordered the Rangers to put their horses in a livery barn and stay there with them. He went to a hotel and didn't go about the Rangers much, but told them to look as near like hay seeds as they could, to keep down suspicion.

A Mr. Grimes, who had been a Ranger, was deputy sheriff at Round Rock, and he and Maurice Moore, who was deputy sheriff in Travis County, had found out what was up and thought they would get the prize, by capturing the Bass party first, if they came in. It was not long before Bass and his men showed up in Round Rock. There was Bass, Underwood, Murphy, Jackson and Seba Barnes, in the band. They tied their horses to a hitching rack back of a store and walked into the store and were casually surveying things, as ranchmen do, when Grimes and Moore entered the store and Grimes said to Bass, "I see you have a six-shooter." Bass replied, "Yes sir, I have two of them," and jerked one out in an instant and shot Grimes dead. Mr. Moore came in behind Grimes, ready to shoot, but Bass was too quick for him, and shot him down, but Moore recovered from his wound, after a long and doubtful chance. Moore was just as game as Bass or any other living man, but he made a mistake.

The Rangers heard the firing, from the barn, and came like shot off a shovel, and got there just as the robbers were mounting their horses. The Rangers opened fire on them, and George Herald shot Seba Barnes through the head just as he was mounting his horse, and Sergeant Dick Ware shot Sam Bass, giving him a mortal wound, but Bass mounted his horse and fled, with Jackson and Underwood. Murphy ran out with them a little distance, but dodged into a lane and came back into Round Rock. The Rangers got their horses as quickly as it could be done and pursued them, but the robbers had reached the brush and thickets and they didn't get them that evening.

Next morning early, Sergeant C. L. Neville took two or three men and was determined to track them up. He got the trail outside of the traveled roads and within two miles, came upon Sam Bass. His horse was tied near him. Bass was lying under a tree and helpless. He spoke to Sergeant Neville first, saying, "I guess I am the man you are looking for. I am Sam Bass." Jackson and Underwood had left him there, knowing he would die, but Bass told them to go. Sergeant Neville cared for Bass the best he could and got him back to Round Rock, where a doctor was gotten to attend him and he lived nearly through that night, making the second night after he was shot. Bass would tell nothing when his inquisitors would try to find out about his men or their doings. He said that what he knew would die with him. Bass gave Sergeant Neville his compass, being the one he traveled by from Nebraska to Texas. Sergeant Neville, being a Company D man, sent the compass to me as a present. George Herald, who killed Seba Barnes, was also a Company D man. Dick Ware, who shot Bass, belonged to another company, but Company D couldn't produce a better man than Ware. Mr. Ware was afterwards a U. S. Marshal for the Western District of Texas.

Underwood and Jackson were never heard of any more in the state of Texas. Murphy in a manner surrendered to Major

Jones, and their agreement was fulfilled to the letter and Murphy left for parts unknown to anyone except Murphy. As to why Murphy did this is only a conjecture, and conjecture rests upon this basis: that his doom rested in a trembling balance. The civil officers of the state, assisted by the Rangers, were going to the bottom of all crime, reaching many cases, that involved the well being of society, and proving their strength to accomplish it. He knew it was only a matter of a short time with him. In another sense, the great secret monitor, called conscience, might have communed with his more noble attributes and told him of the awful wrong he was doing to his brothers and sisters of this world.

I mentioned the Collins brothers as being connected with the Bass gang, in this article. The Collins brothers were cattlemen and well-to-do. Joel Collins was detected in matters connected with Sam Bass and state authorities informed of it. Joel Collins fled to Montana and the deputy sheriff of Fort Worth, in Tarrant County, pursued him. He found Collins in a hotel and demanded his surrender, but Collins was not that kind to do a subservient act, and the sheriff being ready to compel him, had to shoot him. Collins made a few steps through a side door and fell. The sheriff heard him strike the floor with a heavy thud and went to see if he was dead. Collins although dying, had made a quick calculation that he would come, and had a pistol ready, and shot him. The sheriff died first.

The operations of the Bass gang were not known, at least, as the Bass gang, until they were located at Denton, Texas. They worked in different states and many a hold-up and train robbery committed by them was charged to someone else. No confession was ever made by any of them and they all died fighting. What time Bass put in, from Indiana to Texas, or what states he was in, is unknown, but his right name was Bass. We met a gentleman in New Mexico, that taught Sam Bass in school, when he was a small boy.

Since writing the above, I quote from Charles A. Siringo's book, *A Cowboy Detective*:

There is no doubt that Jim T. was a hard case and landed in Montana under an assumed name. Mrs. Julia Landusky gave me many inside facts of Jim T. and his actions when he first landed in the little Rockies, as a slender young man. Now he is a middle aged large, heavy man. Judging from the time he came to the little Rockies, and his description, as given by Mrs. Landusky, Mr. W. L. Dickinson is confident Jim T. is no other than "Dad" Jackson, of the noted Sam Bass gang who robbed the Union Pacific train, near Ogalla, Nebraska in the early 70's. Most of this gang were killed or sent to the penitentiary for this holdup. "Dad" Jackson being the only one that made his getaway. Mr. Dickinson, who was then an operative in the agency, worked on the case.

Considering Results

After the frontier of Texas was practically freed from Indian depredations, there was a turn of thought in the direction of building homes, and utilizing the vast domain gained by that long and sore struggle, which could not be claimed by the Frontier Battalion, except in a sense of sustaining the groundwork of greater men that had left that field in the care of the sons of Texas. The 13th Legislature, and succeeding legislatures took hold of the work like patriots and statesmen and maintained the Battalion as zealously as if they were in the field themselves. Their hearts were there, and willing hands were extended to us, who were in the midst of the work. I have often thought, that the bonds of friendship, so closely woven between the old Texans were knit in the struggles of war, where mutual help brought out the brotherhood of man and the true love of home and family to an extent that few people realize.

The lot of our mothers were cast with our fathers, and their sons and daughters, and taking the whole family, made a unit in the aggregate of Texas loyalty. Loyalty to Texas, was semi-loyalty to the newborn Republic of the United States. The escutcheon on the breast of the American Eagle, was their ideal, in the realm of future hope. The Monroe Doctrine although held subordinate to treaty stipulation, and latent under the surface of diplomacy, was the motor that moved the giant little machine in Texas. A kind of wireless telegraphy was coming from our brothers in the East, to stand by our continental bulwarks. Although we were fighting our battles alone, there were many ears to the ground in the states, to catch the glad sounds of our success. Enough of the heroism of our great leaders have been embalmed in the records of Texas, and jointly preserved in our nation, and in that faith, a succeeding generation in Texas have done the best they could to impart the justice of that faith to posterity.

Texas having succeeded in gaining a government at first hands, gave them a spirit of independence, as well as for independent government. When we were annexed to the United States, we expected protection to our people, which was only partially given, and in truth amounted to little. Then, the independent spirit of Texas asserted itself and brought together the old band that once worshipped the single star. We shouldered the burden of protection with little complaint, but felt a keen injustice in it. But we were compelled to prevent wholesale murder of our people. If any explanation was ever due Texas as to why we didn't get protection, the same is still due, and with interest.

Right here, I will mention some splendid individual effort by officers in the United States service, on the frontier of Texas, in which I delight to honor General Mackenzie, and Lieutenant Bullis. Both were fighters, and their daring deeds will live with Texans, along with the best service of Texas Rangers.

I will not pick a quarrel with as big an hombre as Uncle Sam but his striped breeches did sag on us when we needed help. But the heroic work of the United States Army, in subduing the Indians in other states and territories militates for their neglect in Texas. So we are willing to shake with U. S. soldiers, in any cause or on any ground, within the borders of the United States. And we are also willing to forgive our enemies, the Indians, upon the ground of their belief that we were interlopers and claiming a domain that belonged to them. According to Webster's definition of "domain," it would belong to someone, or some people, by right of occupancy. But, if it was public territory, under no established right of any people who were recognized as a government by other stable governments, it might have been considered as belonging to the Indians, by their occupying it. But in the case of Texas it belonged to Mexico. The red man's claim was not good. I would feel little, if I could not be as magnanimous as Magooshe, the old war chief, on the Mescalero Reservation, who sends me such kind tokens of peace, one of which I copy, sent me by the sutler of that agency, Mr. J. W. Prude:

> Magooshe says he would like to meet you, as a friend and brother once more before he dies. He met you once in battle and you was a brave man and he would like to take your hand, as a friend, since all the world is at peace, so far as he is concerned. And he really means it. I should like to witness the novel meeting of yourself and the old man, after all these years, when I am so familiar with the past history of both men. Yours truly, J. W. Prude.

Since Magooshe has been under control of the U. S. government he has proven to be loyal and I am willing to extend to him the olive branch in the hope of permanent peace.

In the fall of 1882, active work in the line of protection from Indian depredations had almost subsided, as they had learned that there was a big mark along the state border that they must not cross. The builders of the Texas Pacific Railroad were busy at work and had reached the Colorado River, about 150 miles west of Fort Worth. This road ran on the 32nd parallel, straight to El Paso. The distance was about

700 miles, and passed across the northern border of the state, near the Panhandle strip of Texas, set in running north, and joining Kansas and Colorado. The Panhandle was not settled. Settlements had advanced to the north in the state to afford some protection to the men building the railroad and when the road reached the Colorado River, Captain Marsh, of the Frontier Battalion was ordered there with his company, to protect the railroad builders. The road was pushed through to El Paso, and made a sort of dead line to marauding Indians coming from the north.

Their territory was getting smaller, being confined mostly to the Panhandle of Texas, with Kansas, New Mexico and Colorado bordering in. New Mexico, however, was sheltering some of the worst bands that infested Texas. Some of the tribes went to Old Mexico. The Yaqui Indians were on their native heath, in the west of Old Mexico, but have never bothered Texas. The two strongest tribes left in America were Apaches in Arizona, and the Cheyennes in Wyoming. Most of the weaker ones had sought refuge on reservations, in Arizona, New Mexico and other western states.

The service of the Rangers was shifted to the border of Mexico. The thieving and marauding bands were coming back to Texas, sheltered by Mexico but not by the Mexican government, as Mexico was having her own serious troubles with them on her frontier. The United States troops then had to deal with those powerful tribes in Arizona and Wyoming, in which we lost General Custer, General Canby and many other brave men. The United States troops finally killed old Sitting Bull, the leader of the Cheyenne tribe. Old Geronimo, leader of the Apaches, was captured and kept under surveillance until he died about two years ago. Thus we see the approaching end of Cooper's "noble red man." After the several tribes had been brought in on reservations, the policy of the Indian management was to educate the Indian children, and they put many of them in schools far removed from their tribes.

I think this was a mistake, insofar as removing them from their parents to educate them was breaking up the natural ties of family and home, and causing sorrow that their new condition was not ready for. The child pined for its mother and father, and family and the parents loved their children as dearly as the most civilized white people. The children's most absorbing thought was to return to their ties of blood and kindred, which they did after a mechanical training which amounted to nothing more. They went back to the blanket in the tepee, to enjoy God's gift of love in human affection. They could not hope to reach the realm of white society, at a cost of all that is dear to human beings. Whereas, if they had been schooled on their reservations, where the parents could have been in touch and interest with the movement, the parents would have absorbed a great part of the education themselves.

Our own people were unanimous in a hope to civilize them, but that matter was turned over to Eastern people whose actual knowledge of the Indian was gained by dime novel sentiment. It was not an actual knowledge. A board of United States Army officers would have been more competent to deal with the matter from positive knowledge and contact with Indian character, but the military being subordinate to civil authority disqualified them. Placing the Indians on reservations, simply to draw rations and annuities, made indigent sluggards of them, and they took it as a sort of peace offering, to be good. The strong arm of the government was a little too passive in not teaching them to earn a living. However, we recall the action of Lieutenant Stotler, who was Indian agent on the Mescalero reservation in Otero County, New Mexico. Whether this action was upon his own initiative or advised by the management, I do not know. He first rounded them up and had their long hair cut, put hats on them, gave them wagons and teams and farming implements, helped them to pick out good spots of land that could be irrigated, and had a farmer to show them how to sow wheat, plant corn, or any crops they wished to raise. In the fall following their first effort, you could see Mr. Injun driving his team around through the country with grain to sell. Lieutenant Stotler conceived the idea of putting them up a saw mill, as they have plenty of fine timber on their reservations, and the lumber could be used by the government in building and repairing buildings on the agency. The Indians got pay for this work; just imagine a buck Indian cutting and hauling saw logs and working around the mill. Axle grease was substituted for his war paint, and his hatchet had grown to be a chopping axe. They have some cattle, horses, and sheep, and they all use one brand for their stock which is a bow and arrow symbolizing their primitive means of killing game. They still have game on their reservation.

The White Mountain (Sierra Blanco) is on their reservation and the distance around its base is about 50 miles, and well covered with timber up to timber line. The New York World Almanac gives the altitude of the White Mountain 14,145 feet above sea level, being about 100 feet higher than Pike's Peak. The citizens adjacent to the reservation get along nicely with the Indians. I received a letter a few days ago from their old war chief in which he stated that he wished to see me, and shake my hand cordially, adding that he was once wild and mean, but is so no more. I answered him, that I would like to see him and shake before we passed to the happy hunting ground.

In rounding up our service, through a period of nearly seven years, we lost only one man killed in action. Several of our men had their hats and clothes punctured with bullets, and some horses killed and wounded. Our manner of fighting was quick work, at close range. Only a few minutes was decisive. The enemy had no time to look for advantage, and once they broke their line for retreat, they could never rally under constant fire. We suffered most in the Deer Creek Fight, which is mentioned in one of the first chapters of this writing, but that fight just preceded our service in the Frontier Battalion.

MY MEN ARE CRACK SHOTS AND I AM NOT AFRAID OF THEM GETTING THE WORST OF ANYTHING.

-CAPT. JOHN A. BROOKS

FENCE CUTTERS

After we had helped to make investments safe in Texas we found that the man with capital was watching our progress, and didn't fail to cinch what we had fought for, in buying and leasing great bodies of land to run cattle on. This land was fenced with barbed wire. Many men on the frontier, who thought they were helping to conserve a public interest in the public domain of Texas, began to see that capital had shut out all small interests, and the door of opportunity was closed. It was not generally Texas capital that did this, but the state was lax in not protecting its own sovereignty. Nearly all frontiersmen were poor in purse, having been depleted by a history of robbery by Indians and outlaws. The capitalists resented fencing them out, but they did it in a way that made criminals of them under the law. Frontiersmen commenced to cut those fences, regardless of law, but were not a match to the situation. Consequently, they were down and out. They had to hunt new territory to make a start. Texas was liberal to capital, but all her people didn't share her liberality, in a measure that they had earned.

We do not mean to controvert a former statement in this writing, that Texas was liberal in giving people homes, but a home on the frontier, that didn't combine stock raising was a poor home. Her endowment of public land, to schools and universities, also her asylums and other institutions, was simply grand. But the people on the frontier were very remote from those blessings, notwithstanding they occupied the ground included in those magnanimous donations. They all felt a pride in this, but to give capital, which was cold-blooded, advantage against them, the rope and noose to strangle them with, was very apparent to even a frontiersman. The little neglected citizenship on the frontier was too insignificant to be heard in legislation, and in consequence they had to take what followed.

Equal opportunity was the boon they asked. Did they get it? No, they got epithets piled high on them, as law breakers and undesirable citizens, and had to subside as felons. It was not only the fence cutters, but all the small stock owners, that received the cold warning to keep off the grass. Texas could make no distinction in the rights of her citizens, by law, and failed to see that natural rights were involved. Consequently, men from other states were watching our fight, with about as much interest in it, as they would have in a Kilkenny cat fight until our affairs were adjusted to warrant investment. Sam Houston and his compatriots left a legacy in land to Texas, that made her as rich as Croesus, but could not live long enough to conserve it. However, the Republic of Texas began right, in granting what they called a headright, giving to the head of a family a certain amount of land, as a recognition of their services in fighting for it.

In 1874, the land on the Texas frontier covered about the same area that the well-settled portion of the state covered, if not more, including the Panhandle strip, and from San Antonio to the Rio Grande, and up and down that river, for nearly a thousand miles. That frontier territory has proven that it was worth as much to Texas as her cotton farms. It has stocked nearly every state, west of the Mississippi River to California, with cattle. It built Texas a capitol building that cost six million dollars. It subsidized the M. K. & T. railroad, in a vast donation, also other railroads. It built up other Texas institutions to perfect grandeur, and Texas has reserved land enough for schools, to give her the largest school fund of any state in the Union, based upon population of scholastic age. But the poor fellows that made the land available only got a little mock turtle soup.

THAT SHOWED THE KIND OF LOVE CAPTAIN MCNELLY HAD FOR HIS
MEN, AND HE DID NOT HAVE A MAN IN HIS COMPANY THAT WOULDN'T
HAVE STEPPED IN BETWEEN HIM AND DEATH.

-RANGER WILLIAM C. CALLICOTT

Horrel War

I denominate this a "war" because the Horrels were the principal actors in what was called the Lincoln County War in New Mexico.

In 1867, when Texas was trying to rebuild her torn up government under a guard of United States soldiers, Edmund J. Davis was elected governor of Texas. Governor Davis commanded a regiment in the Union Army, although a Texan, and his regiment was composed of Texans. While Reconstruction was going on, Governor Davis put out a State Police to keep down disorders until civil government could be established. He appointed Capt. Tom Williams as captain of police. Captain Williams served with Governor Davis in the Union Army.

The Horrels lived in Lampasas County, Texas, there being three or four brothers of them, and all being old settlers there they had many friends. I do not believe they had smelled much blood in real conflict—not at least to the extent which makes opposing forces friends in mutual admiration of courage. They were very zealous in keeping up strife over the dead war issues and caused much trouble in Lampasas County. Captain Williams was dispatched to Lampasas to quell the disturbances. The Horrels were defiant and considered Captain Williams an intruder into their dominion and openly murdered him. This put the United States soldiers after them.

They dodged from place to place until it got too warm for them, when they left for New Mexico. They came to where the city of Roswell is now located, and there being no law in the territory then, except military, and that only in spots, they had a clear field to work in.

In 1868 some big cattle ranches were being established in the country, and in the latter part of that year John Chisum started his big ranch on South Spring River, four miles south of Roswell. Soon after that, Billy the Kid started a little war of his own up in Lincoln County; and the details of that being too tedious to write, it need only be said that murder and robbery were its leading features. Mr. Chisum found that fighting men were in demand to protect his cattle; and the Kid bunch and the Horrels being the strongest and they together having absorbed about all the fighting characters in the country, he had to use some fine diplomacy in securing one or the other, or both, to help him out. I have been told that fighting wages didn't satisfy them and that they appropriated Mr. Chisum's cattle very freely to make up the deficit.

The Horrels were not common thieves, but necessity had driven them to do things of a lawless character that made outlaws of them. They became very desperate men. They killed several Mexican citizens in Lincoln County.

After their several years' stay in New Mexico, democracy had been restored to voting power in Texas and Richard Coke was elected governor, and the Horrels made the mistake of going back to Lampasas County. A Democratic administration had to deal out justice to them for the murder of Captain Williams and some other men. In the meantime, the Ranger force had been put into the field by Governor Coke and political sympathy didn't figure with them. The civil officers were still unable to cope with the situation there and the Rangers were called on for help. Major Jones went in person and took my old duty, sergeant N. O. Reynolds, with him in command of the squad. I loved Major Jones, but he played an Irish trick on me when he took Reynolds from me. But I was compensated later on when the Major secured a Captain's commission for Reynolds.

The Horrels were known to be in Lampasas County, but they were kept posted as to the movements of the Rangers. On the other hand, the good citizens were trying just as hard to locate them for the Rangers. In a neighborhood some eight or ten miles south of the town of Lampasas the people got positive information that the Horrels were fifteen or twenty miles southeast of the town, on the Lampasas River. Now, to get this information to Major Jones might appear to be a small matter, but the Horrels had spies on every road leading in their direction. There was a young fellow from the east, the veriest tenderfoot, visiting in that neighborhood. He told them that he would deliver that message to Major Jones. They saw that he had the backbone to try it and they let him go with it. That young man was J. M. Hawkins, who is now postmaster in Alamogorda, New Mexico. Sure enough, their spies rounded him up on the road, but I imagine Hawkins tried to appear greener than he really was, playing the baby act successfully, and went on his way rejoicing. He delivered the message to Major Jones.

This located the Horrels and no time was lost in starting the Rangers after them. It was on a rainy evening and the Horrels had sought shelter in a vacant house near the river. Some of the most bitter enemies of the Horrels wanted to go with Sergeant Reynolds and assist in capturing them, but Reynold's declined their help except to take one man with him to show him the house they were in. When he got near this house he told his man to go back as he needed no further assistance. Reynolds advanced cautiously, in the night, and encountered no guard or watchman in his approach. The Horrels were all asleep in the house. Reynolds placed his men around the house with orders not to shoot until he ordered them to do so. He opened the front door and walked into the house alone. He lighted a match and saw the situation in the front room and had to act at a flash, as Tom Horrel was sleeping in that room with his rifle on the bed with him. He saw Reynolds by the light of the match, and Reynolds saw his gun—both men grabbed the gun at the same time.

The Horrels were big, powerful men, and while Reynolds was no less powerful, he didn't look it. In the scuffle over the gun, the weapon was discharged. The men in front pushed into the house and in that crucial moment Reynolds told them not to shoot—that the discharge of the gun was an accident. Reynolds wrenched the gun out of Horrel's hands and told him they were the Rangers. The men in the other room had made no demonstrations so far, knowing that if they ran out they would meet bullets. Reynolds talked Tom Horrel into calmness and told him to go into the other rooms and tell his men to come out and surrender and he would see that they were not mobbed. Horrel had met the one man in his life that was the finest of steel, and he appeared to like Reynolds from that moment. Tom went in and told them and vouched for it himself that they would not be mobbed. They all came out and surrendered to the Rangers. They were taken up to the town of Lampasas and no considerable crowd of men were allowed to come near them.

Major Jones, conferring with the civil authorities, knew it would not do to put them in the Lampasas jail, and they were sent to a jail some 100 miles north of there, thinking they would escape mob violence. When Reynolds parted with them at the jail the Horrels shed tears and told him they never expected to see him again.

The Rangers were kept at Lampasas awhile, and as long as they were there the Horrels were pretty safe, notwithstanding they were some distance away.

As soon, however, as they were taken from Lampasas a mob was organized which was sufficiently strong to go to the jail where the Horrels were incarcerated. They overpowered the sheriff, entered the jail and shot the Horrels to death.

The ugly crime was never righted by law.

HE RELISHED CAMP LIFE IMMENSELY. HE HAD NOTHING TO DO BUT TO ENJOY LIFE. RANGERS WERE NEVER SICK—THEY COULD ENDURE ANY AMOUNT OF EXPOSURE AND KEPT IN PERFECT HEALTH.

-MRS. LUVENIA CONWAY ROBERTS ON THE LIFE
OF THE FRONTIER BATTALION'S SURGEON

Adios, Rangers

In the fall of 1882, we found ourselves becoming inactive, as our primary work abated, in a sense that was gratifying to our past effort, in the frontier service. The Indian question had principally been settled in Texas, and the burden now rested in other states and territories. The Ranger force was being reduced by the state, and it appeared to us that we were only looking after odds and ends. Consequently I tendered my resignation as captain of Company D, Frontier Battalion to our Adjutant General, W. H. King.

Adjutant General King, feeling very friendly to me, in answer, asked me to take command of a company of Rangers at Fort Davis, which would have been following our common enemy, to the border of Mexico. But Company D was our idol, and the health of my wife demanded my most serious attention. General King accepted my resignation. He was a tried and true soldier, and a man of rare ability. We parted from him reluctantly, as we did from our old company, and to the survivors of my old company, we offer a farewell to last to the shores of eternity.

Since my goodbye to the Rangers I will try to tell something about the great state that some of them still live in.

Texas is more diversified, in climate and soils, than probably any other State in the Union of States. Mainly on account of her various altitudes, from the Gulf, to a point opposite the Rocky Mountains in Colorado.

The physical geography of the state connects a western arid belt with a semi-humid belt, lying or being below the

32nd parallel and all north of that is arid land. The Texas Pacific Railroad runs east and west, on the 32nd parallel. Those zones run north and south, and connect near the middle of the state, their blending is almost as fine as the colors of the rainbow.

We will draw an imaginary line north and south from Big Springs on the Texas Pacific Railroad running south, say 30 miles west of Austin, and crossing the Guadalupe River just below Seguin, and running straight to Goliad, on the San Antonio River, thence by Beeville and to Corpus Christi. This line crosses all the rivers mentioned diagonally.

We will cross-section the eastern division, by giving the character of land, and its products, only giving staple products as a basis.

We will draw a line from Big Springs south to Fort Mason, in Mason County, a distance of nearly two hundred miles, thence east via Lampasas Springs to Waco, on the Brazos River, thence east by Fairfield to Pine Bluff, on the Trinity River. Thence north to the thirty-second parallel east of Dallas. We will have to take in six or seven counties lying north of Dallas and Fort Worth, as the best wheat, corn and oats counties in the State. The block we have lined in produces fine cotton, corn, wheat, and oats. Commencing again at Pine Bluff, on the Trinity River, and running east to the Sabine River, joining Louisiana, and north to the Indian Territory, we have a timbered section, which give us lumber in the west. This section is generally denominated Eastern Texas.

We will now take another block from the town of Mason south to Seguin on the Guadalupe River, thence east to the city of Houston and still east to Orange on the Sabine River, with slight variance in crop production, only a gain in cotton, with oat crop lighter on account of rust in the oats.

Now we come to the coast block, from Corpus Christi, east to Port Arthur, taking in all the zigzags of peninsulas, bays and inlets on the Texas coasts, embracing the cities of Galveston, Houston, and smaller coast towns.

We will now take up five counties near the middle of the coast block, namely, Colorado, Wharton, Matagorda, Fort Bend and Harris, as producers of rice, sugar, corn, cotton, and nearly all crops desired. This block of counties embrace the famous Old Caney lands, which are noted for sugar cane, (ribbon cane) and you have to almost climb the cotton stalks to pick the cotton, and the truth is big enough without exaggeration. Taking east and west of this block the land is generally good, and produces finely.

I am not boosting for Texas, and more, I do not believe in that method of deception that lures people to the promised land to find themselves victims of graft. Texas has its drawbacks just the same as any other state, which are drouths, and late frosts in the spring, with mosquitoes in the coast country, quite enough to be interesting.

We now take up the "Western Hemisphere," allowing Texas to be a little world.

In the arid belt lying west of what we have attempted to describe, lay the great cattle ranges of the state, and from the coast to her northern boundary. The indigenous grasses of western Texas are many, and very nutritious, having fattening qualities of blue grass or timothy, but they have to struggle for life, against weeds, where the ranges are eaten out by overstocking. Big pastures having been fenced in by private enterprise, has preserved the grass to some extent, as individuals look after their interests, in *not* overstocking. Within the last decade, irrigation has attracted the people and caused them to see its great value. About one-third of this vast area is farming land, provided it can be reached with water. Several self-flowing canals and ditches have been made, and many pumping plants installed, in this arid region. They lie west of the Norther (north wind) belt, and are almost immune from freezes, which fact makes that section ideal for farming, taking climate as a factor.

Now we will talk about our neighbors. Many Texans don't know that one of the hardest fought battles that ever occurred on Texas soil was fought by a few ragged Missourians, under command of Colonel Donophin, in 1846. This occurred right where the city of El Paso is now situated. This was on his march to Mexico to join General Scott. You will find the particulars of this in Colonel Ralph Emerson Twitchel's history of the Spanish and American occupation of New Mexico. We think that Texas historians have taken too much for granted, that this piece of history is embraced in the Mexican war history. It was fought on Texas soil, by Missourians, not yet under the immediate command of General Scott. We all know that Colonel Donophin was fighting the northern division of the Mexican army, but Texas was more directly interested in this fight.

Colonel Donophin was a thousand miles from any base of supplies. The great statesman, Thomas H. Benton of Missouri, had his ear to the ground listening for Donophin, but he had gone too far from him to send any tidings. The storms and prairie fires had obliterated Donophin's trail across the great plains, and when this fight occurred, he had no carrier dove to tell where he was. He pulled down the bars of northern Mexico, and marched in on a dirt road strewn with cactus, far out into the interior of Mexico, where he met General Scott. His men were almost in a nude condition, but they were as gay as colts, and each one of them felt that he was as big a man as General Scott, on a basis of American pride. Hence, the saying that you have to show a Missourian that he can't do a thing.

The early settlers of Texas almost perfectly typify early colonial life in Virginia, varying in, or under the auspices of which the undertaking was made. The early colonial life in Virginia were under the ban of imperial surveillance, and all their first charters of institutions that appeared too liberal to the King of Great Britain, were revoked, putting them back under the yoke of truckling subjects. The analogy of, or between the settling of the two great states, relate more to the character of the people. In fact many of the first settlers of Texas were the same people, or descended straight from them. Their independence and hospitality were an Old Virginia product. Linking them back through all the states, to Virginia, the first Texans simply came on the crest of the first wave west. Kentucky furnished a big quota, with their old brindle rifles, and many old Texans are yet adepts in handling a corkscrew. I hope their hoary old heads may think kindly of this mention of them. I ask the readers of this small effort to have patience with a novice, and if I have failed to interest you it will be a failure of truth, as I saw it, by bitter experience, and pleasure mixed.

Excerpts from the memoirs of Mrs. D. W. Roberts,
published in 1928 under the title

A Woman's
Reminiscences
of
SIX YEARS
IN CAMP
WITH THE
TEXAS RANGERS

.

THEN, THE INDEPENDENT SPIRIT OF TEXAS ASSERTED ITSELF &
BROUGHT TOGETHER THE OLD BAND THAT ONCE WORSHIPPED THE
SINGLE STAR.
                    -CAPT. D. W. ROBERTS

IN CAMP WITH TEXAS RANGERS

M enard is situated on the beautiful San Saba River. It contained only a few houses in 1875, and most of them were made of cedar pickets, had dirt floors and no spare room. We were fortunate to find one house with three rooms. The family that occupied it numbered seven, but they were kind enough to spare us one room. That was frontier hospitality. The room was small and had space for only one bed and a chair. It contained no window and no mirror. There was a wash basin on the porch that served for all.

The Rangers required only a few days to prepare quarters for us. About fifty yards from their camp stood a portion of a camp house. It had a shingle roof and a rock floor. It was converted into a kitchen, size twenty by twenty feet. Gunny sacks were tacked upon the walls. For our bedroom the Rangers built a room of logs with walls three feet high, on top of which they put a tent. It was provided with a fireplace built of stone. The floor was carpeted with gunny sacks. The kitchen also served as a storeroom. It was all so cozy. Here the newly-weds began housekeeping.

The camp was located in a fine pecan grove on the river about two miles below Menard. I wish I could describe that country as it was at that time. Beautiful nature had not been marred by the hand of man. It seemed to belong to the birds and wild animals, they were so abundant. There was game of every description. I had fished many times in the Colorado River and in Eagle Lake, but had never caught a fish. When

151

I threw my hook into the beautiful San Saba almost immediately it was seized by a nice catfish. It was thrilling.

Another pleasure I had in anticipation was horseback
riding. I had never ridden horseback at Columbus, but my
sweetheart wrote me that he had a fine saddle horse for me.
Before leaving that place, I had made an up-to-date riding
habit which extended below the feet from half a yard to a
yard. In 1875 no part of a woman's leg was visible. Looking
back I recall a vivid picture of myself on my first horseback
ride. Perched upon a sidesaddle, with a habit reaching almost
to the ground, I set out. We rode along a trail through a thick
wood. Captain Roberts led the way. Suddenly he stopped,
drew his pistol and motioned for me to stop. I thought, of
course, that we had come upon Indians. After he had fired the
second time, I saw wild turkeys fly. We took two back to camp
with us. What do you suppose happened to my riding habit
passing through that brush? It was so badly torn that I had to
cut off so much of it that what remained barely covered my
feet. It was much more convenient, but it required great care
not to expose an ankle, which would have been scandalous.

I was now a regular member of Company D, but entirely
unarmed. I spoke to the Captain about how embarrassing it
was not to have a gun and not to be able to protect myself
in case of an attack. He immediately purchased a .22 caliber
Remington rifle. I practiced target shooting with the Rangers
until I was satisfied that I could shoot as well as any of them,
and could kill game, of which there was an abundance.

My ride through the brush showed that I did not have suitable clothes for hunting. I sent to Austin for a hunting suit
made of heavy material, for I was particularly fond of hunting
and fishing. I was warned daily of the danger of going too
far from camp, but my interest in fishing caused me to forget

about danger. On one occasion when I had gone some distance from camp, I discovered ten horsemen coming down the trail in single file. I had often heard that that was the way the Indians traveled. There was no doubt in my mind that they were Indians. I struck a bee line for camp, expecting every minute to be murdered. I knew it was useless to run, nevertheless I struck a lively gait. Looking back over my shoulder, to my great relief I saw them stop to water their horses. They were Mexicans. I had my gun by me, but it never occurred to me to use it in case of an attack. After that experience I was more careful.

Life in camp did not deprive me of visitors. The pioneer women came to see me and made me feel welcome among them. Many of them were educated and refined; those that had been deprived of those advantages nevertheless had hearts of gold. Friendships formed in those days have stood the test of half a century. There were some charming young ladies in Menard—every one of them a belle. There were about ten boys to one girl. Whenever Captain Roberts was called away from camp, I would invite one of the young ladies to stay with me. The Rangers paid them much mind, and had many excuses for calling at our camp to get a look at a pretty girl.

The frontier people were not without their social pleasures. Amusements were not frequent nor were they elaborate, but they were enjoyed all the more because they came so seldom. I recall spending a very enjoyable day at a quilting bee. While the fingers plied the needle, tongues were equally busy. At noon all repaired to the dining room, which also served as kitchen. The table groaned under the burden of rations tempting to the appetite. The feast lasted as long as we were there. When twilight began to fall the young men gathered in for a dance. And a dance it was. Few indulged in the round dance, as the old time square dance was most popular. The table extended its inviting savor, and one could go in and help himself between dances. The beverage was steaming hot coffee. The dance lasted until daylight. Many came from long distances, and then it was an Indian country. I did not spend the night, for I had Ranger protection and went home at midnight.

Company D was composed of a superior class of men. Some of them belonged to the first families of Austin; for example, Captain James B. Gillett, author of *Six Years with the Texas Rangers*; Rube Anderson, stepson of Adjutant General John B. Jones; Thurlow Weed, brother of Mr. V. O. Weed; Charlie Nevill, later Captain Nevill; Grooms Lee, J. W. Bell, the Sieker brothers from Baltimore (L. P. Sieker succeeded Captain Roberts in command of Company D), W. W. Lewis of Menard, and R. R. Russell of San Antonio. I will not attempt to name all, but mention a few who are well known to residents of Austin. But these are indicative of the class of men in our company.

Every member of Company D was devoted to Captain Roberts, and during the entire time we were in the service each did all he could to make us comfortable in camp. I recall with feelings of gratitude the many acts of kindness that were shown us.

The Rangers supplied me with various pets. Among them were squirrels, prairie dogs, a cub bear, a dog, and a canary bird. I enjoyed the bear while he was little, but he got cross as he grew up and I turned him loose. We were never dull in camp. Several of the Rangers were musical, and had their instruments with them. Captain Roberts was a fine violinist. A race track was laid out and there was horse racing. Card playing was not allowed and it was not done openly. Betting on horse races was permitted, but the Rangers ran their races for amusement. We had a croquet set, and that game was enjoyed.

After we had been in camp a few months it was decided to go up the river about thirty miles, which meant that far from any settlement. Going into that wild country exposed us to encounters with Indians. A strong guard—ten men— was taken along. That number had been victorious in their last fight with Indians, so we felt well protected. After we had made our new camp, and before we commenced to fish, it was agreed that we would not scatter and that everyone would keep his gun by him. Such sport as we enjoyed! As fast as a hook could be cast it would be caught up by a fish. I have often wondered whether a white man had ever fished there before us. We spent two pleasant days. No live Indians were seen, but we found the skeleton of a dead one where he had been buried in a crevice of rock. When we returned to camp, I felt that I had been on a scout, and I have always had a suspicion that it was so reported to headquarters, but this I do not know to be a fact.

Their encounters with the Rangers had taught the Indians to be cautious. Before the Rangers were stationed at Menard, Indians raided every light of the moon, stealing horses and murdering anyone they met on their way out. Captain Rufe Perry commanded Company D during the first six months after it was organized. I must tell you what a brave wife he had. She visited him while he was encamped right on the trail where the Indians crossed the river. One beautiful, moonlit night ten Indians passed right by his camp. She stayed there alone while Captain Perry reported the presence of the Indians to the main camp. That was a wife for a Ranger! Captain Perry detailed a scout, commanded by Lt. Roberts, to pursue the Indians. In the fight that ensued, Lt. Roberts captured the shield of an Indian chief who was killed. He presented it to his friend, Alex Casparis, whose widow still has it.

After this fight with the Rangers, the Indians were more cautious. They abandoned their favorite ford on the river. However, the news that Indians had been killed struck terror to the hearts of some of the more timid. The latter feared that the Indians would come in great numbers and murder all the whites in a spirit of revenge. They visited Captain Roberts and said, "Oh, Captain, the Indians will murder us all." He assured them that fear was the only thing an Indian could be taught.

A number of people came to camp to see the Indian prisoner. It was contrary to orders to take prisoners, but as Captain Roberts states in his book, he could not kill a man, even an Indian, when he was begging for his life. The prisoner suffered agony from fear while in camp, and his expression showed that he expected momentarily to be killed. At Austin the Indian prisoner was given a ride in a city carriage. He expressed his pleasure by repeating the word *bonito*. Within two years he died in the penitentiary of tuberculosis.

We had been in camp at Menard only a short time when a report was brought in that Scott Cooley was in the neighborhood. Captain Roberts at once detailed a scout, himself taking command. I was greatly alarmed. I knew Scott Cooley's reputation as a killer, and I could not believe that the Rangers would be able to arrest him without some being killed. Captain Roberts tried to remove my fears by assuring me that that class of men did not have true courage and that he had never found it difficult to arrest them. However, I was not easy until all had returned to camp. If Cooley had been at Menard he had made good his escape. False reports were not uncommon due to unintentional mistakes. It still appears remarkable to me that during the entire period of Captain Roberts' command of Company D not one of his men was killed by Indians and only one (George Bingham) was killed by outlaws.

PAY DAY

The Rangers were paid at the end of each quarter. It was necessary for the captain of the company to go to Austin for the money. That was in "the good old days" when there were few banks. As I have stated above, it was a four days' journey from Menard to Austin. We set out early in December with a guard of two men, whose homes were in Austin. The first night we spent at Mason Hotel. The war was over and everything was quiet and serene. It was pleasant to meet again acquaintances formed during the stormy times of my first visit. Our next stop was at the Nimitz Hotel, the best hotel in West Texas at that time; it has maintained its reputation down to the present time.

We planned to spend the third night at Dripping Springs, but the best laid plans of mice and men, etc. It commenced raining at ten in the forenoon and continued for about three hours. The roads were soon so bad that it was clear that it would be impossible to reach Dripping Springs that afternoon. None of the men knew of any place where we could find shelter for the night. We were not prepared to camp. Finally, we met a boy riding a horse; he had no saddle, only a rope for a bridle, and wore a white hat whose brim was turned under on either side so that it was pointed. He told us that he lived about two miles away and that he could direct us to his house. He took the lead; we followed. For some cause Captain Roberts and the Rangers commenced asking the boy questions in regard to what they had to eat. It may have been his appearance, or they may have been hungry. They kept on until the boy told them that his people had nothing to eat but "taters." He said his father had gone to Fredericksburg after flour. That was discouraging, and when we got to the house, there was no room, and the children piled out of the door like sheep. Captain Roberts remarked to his Rangers, "Boys, this is a ground hog case; we have to camp." We congratulated ourselves that the weather was warm. We had our coats, and each had a blanket. The Captain and I occupied the back, and the boys lay down on the wet ground.

Were you ever on a bleak hill when a blue Texas norther came up? Well, that is what happened to us that night. We almost froze to death. When one of the Rangers lay down, the other called to him, "Get up and die like a man." As soon as they could see to harness the mules, we set out and arrived at Dripping Springs at nine o'clock. The wife of Captain Roberts' brother gave us an excellent breakfast, which we certainly enjoyed. After thawing out, we proceeded to Austin, glad to meet our friends.

I found it impossible to convince my friends that camp life could be attractive, and they could not understand how I could be content to live in a tent. We enjoyed the few days in Austin very much, but when the time came to go back to camp I was quite eager to go. Living close to nature had its pleasures and benefits that far outweighed the privations. On our return trip the weather was good and we had good hotel accommodations each night.

The Rangers were glad to see us arrive safely with their pay. A Ranger's pay was forty dollars a month. Besides, everything was furnished him, except his clothing, which was not expensive. Rangers wore civilian clothes suitable for their work. There was nothing at Menard to tempt a young man to spend his money. Even girls were not expensive then; the only things a young man could buy for his girl was stick candy, gum drops, and chewing gum. The question then arises, What did a Ranger do with his money? Some of them invested in cattle. R. R. "Dick" Russell and others invested in that business while they were in the service. They had friends who looked after their livestock, and when their term of service expired they had a good start. Dick Russell became a millionaire. The Sieker brothers invested in ranch property. Many others made good investments. Then there were others whose money got away from them, leaving nothing to show for it; for, while gambling was prohibited, it could not be entirely suppressed.

Soon after our return to camp, we were visited by the Major of the Battalion, John B. Jones. The Battalion comprised six companies, and the Major visited them in turn. He was much beloved by all, and his visits were looked forward to with much pleasure. He was always accompanied by the battalion surgeon, Dr. Nicholson. Dr. Nicholson was a typical Southern gentleman; the kind one reads about in novels. He relished camp life immensely. He had nothing to do but to enjoy life. Rangers were never sick—they could endure any amount of exposure, and kept in perfect health.

Our Major favored me; when supplies were sent, there was always a box directed to "Lieutenant Roberts, Assistant Commander of Company D," that was filled with fruit and other delicacies. Of this box I took possession…

TOUR OF DUTY IN SOUTH TEXAS

After spending two months in San Antonio, I was delighted to receive a message from my husband telling me to join him at Sabinal. I took the first stagecoach out. Captain Roberts had come on in advance of the company, and we boarded in Sabinal until the Rangers arrived and established camp twelve miles below the town. Three families resided at Sabinal, so we were fortunate in finding a place to board. I was glad to get back to camp.

We found that a very different country from Menard. Game was not so abundant. Fishing was good, but not as good as at Menard. It was not the frontier that we loved so well.

Our camp was in a beautiful live oak grove, and there we spent the winter of 1877-78. The Indians made no raids while we were there, but the Rangers had plenty to do running down outlaws. Many arrests were made. The wives of some of the married prisoners camped near us in order to be near their husbands. They were permitted to talk to their husbands only in the presence of a guard. The innocent suffered with the guilty. They may have been good women. It must have been heartrending to them to see their husbands in shackles. I pitied them. But nature is cruel, and they were victims of that law. In the good old days marriage was binding. A woman who valued her reputation would endure almost anything rather than be dubbed a grass widow. I believe in divorces, and am glad to see the change, but regret that they have become so numerous…

In the spring Captain Roberts received orders from Major Jones to break camp and travel under secret orders. Now, that was exciting; to go and not know where we were going. The first day we traveled north. Sitting around the campfire, the Rangers discussed the next day's march. Some adventurous chap suggested that we might not stop short of New York City. The earth was carpeted with beautiful flowers. Dewberries were ripe. We made it convenient to camp near some house where there was a pen full of calves so that we would be able to obtain cream. We progressed by easy stages, allowing ourselves plenty of time to gather dewberries and to enjoy the wildflowers and beautiful scenery. Thus we continued until we arrived at Austin. The Rangers camped near the city, and we visited with our friends. The trip from Sabinal to Austin was the most enjoyable I have ever taken, excepting our bridal tour.

After resting at Austin for a few days, we again received orders to proceed, but this time we knew where we were going. I had known all the time, but did not dare to tell.

Camp on the San Saba

C aptain Roberts was ordered to take his company to Menard County and to establish his camp on the San Saba River five miles below Fort McKavett. Fort McKavett was located on the San Saba River twenty miles above our former camp. The trip from Austin to Menard was uneventful. On arriving at our destination, we pitched our tents under some beautiful oaks.

Up to this time we had had only one tent and a kitchen, but at Camp San Saba we were supplied a second tent, which because of its size the Rangers named The Elephant. We felt that our household was growing. The Elephant I furnished as my guest chamber, and equipped it with army cot, washstand, a small table, and a mirror hung on the tent pole. Our kitchen was built of logs, with a tent for a roof. Both our tents were floored—we had outgrown gunny-sack floor covering. The two tents and kitchen were surrounded by a brush fence, with a whitewashed gate that looked quite imposing. The State furnished us a cook. The rations issued to the Rangers included only the substantials, but were of such generous quantity that we had a surplus to exchange for butter, milk, eggs, etc. Honey was obtained from bee trees. Game and fish were abundant.

The Rangers and the Yankee soldiers were now neighbors. The soldiers at Fort McKavett had never furnished protection against Indian depredations. Had they afforded such protection, Company D would not have been sent there. The soldiers did not go after the Indians the way the Rangers did. Their movements were military, regulated by a lot of red tape, and they couldn't catch them. The Rangers used no ceremony; they mounted their horses, ran down the Indians and killed them. The soldiers received thirteen dollars a month; the Rangers received forty dollars. When a soldier wished to quit the service before his enlistment expired the only way out was to desert; when a Ranger wanted to quit, his commander would readily give him a discharge on the ground that a dissatisfied Ranger was not efficient. Rangers had their hearts in the service—they were protecting the frontier of their home State. Soldiers and officers had no social intercourse; Rangers visited at captain's headquarters, and were frequently invited to a meal.

The officers at the fort were friendly, and one of them said to Captain Roberts, "Your fights here in the shadow of this post are so humiliating that I feel like resigning." On my visit to the post I met my first house guest, Miss Cora Ogden of San Antonio. She was visiting her brother, who was sutler. She was a charming young lady. I entertained her by taking her hunting and fishing. There was always a Ranger who would volunteer to go with us, get the bait and bait the hooks. We took a good many rides behind mules and regretted very much that we could not ride horseback. Unfortunately there was but one sidesaddle and one habit available—it would have been impossible to have ridden a man's saddle without exposing an ankle. Some evenings we visited the main camp to listen to the string band.

The Rangers and the military exchanged courtesies in the following manner: The officers and their wives would drive down to our camp to listen to our string band, and we would go up and hear their brass band.

Soon after Miss Ogden returned to the post, I was fishing alone, with my rifle by my side, when I saw a beaver swimming near the opposite bank of the river. I had never killed any large game. I wanted to get that beaver, but felt it would be useless to try to kill him with my .22 rifle. So I trusted to finding him next day, and in the meantime I would get Captain Roberts' gun. The next afternoon about the same hour I took a Winchester and returned to the same spot on the river to watch for the beaver. The sun was down before he appeared. I fired a Winchester for the first time, but I killed him. He sank at once, and I was greatly disappointed, fearing that I would not get him after all. Captain Roberts assured me that we would recover him. Early next morning we went to the river. The beaver had risen and my husband fished him out for me. Beaver were shedding at that season, so the fur was useless, but the tail went to London. I had made the acquaintance of a young Englishwoman at the post. She was soon to return to her home in London, and insisted on taking the tail as a souvenir of the Texas frontier.

The Rangers were kept quite busy during the summer, scouting for Indians. However, they found time to stage a minstrel performance at Menard. The citizens of that place were planning to build a church; the Rangers gave the play for their benefit. They cleared sixty dollars, which was the first cash contribution to the church building fund. My guest chamber was frequently occupied, for I enjoyed the company of young ladies. It was fun to visit the big camp and watch the rehearsals. The manager of the play was able to select some good talent. Sometimes the boys would attend a dance at Menard; on such occasions there was "rustling" for clothes. The Captain would sometimes lend a suit, and the others would invariably tell the girls about it.

Practical jokes varied camp life. Even I caught the spirit. The Rangers were always on the anxious seat when the Legislature assembled to make the biennial appropriations. Would the appropriations for the Rangers be continued? Would they all be continued in the service? The mail was looked forward to with great eagerness at such times. Captain Roberts was away one day when the mail was brought. There was a letter to him from the Adjutant General. The Rangers came to me to know what the letter contained. I read it to them correctly that the appropriation had been made, but I added, "Discharge every man under five feet ten." Then there was some measuring. When Captain Roberts returned and read the letter to them, they knew I had manufactured that last statement, but they did not hold it against me.

Each quarter Captain Roberts made the trip to Austin for the Rangers' pay, and I accompanied him. Most of these trips were uneventful, but they afforded enjoyable visits to our friends. But the trip I am going to tell about now was different. It rained all day between Mason and Fredericksburg. We found it impossible to reach the Nimitz Hotel by night. As we knew of no place where we could find shelter for the night we were worried. Fortunately, we met a man who told us that at the end of the next mile we would find a trail which would lead us to a house. It was dark when we reached the house. A woman met us, and kindly consented to give us lodging. She at once began apologizing to me, or rather explaining why they were so poor. She said, "All my children are gals. We might get along better if *he* would stay at home and work, but *he* has to be gone away all the time preaching."

The house was one long room. It was occupied by two families. Each had a separate fireplace, and each had several children. Our hostess prepared our supper by cooking some corn dodgers in a skillet, and by frying some bacon in the same skillet—the only cooking vessel she had. She gave us some black coffee. The table seated four, which was our number. After supper our hostess pointed out the bed we were to occupy, which was in a row with several others. There were no partitions and no curtains. Undressing was a public affair. If the present style of dress had been in vogue then, undressing would have been a simple thing, but in those days we wore clothes. I managed the best I could. Soon after we retired "he" came home.

While "he" was partaking of the evening meal "he" said, "I hear a lot about hard times when I'm gone, but I never see it until I come home." It was with great difficulty that I restrained myself from getting up and choking him. I wanted to say, "You lazy, trifling thing, running around, eating hot biscuits and fried chicken; and your family starving!"...

Our next meal after leaving the preacher's house was at Nimitz Hotel. How hungry we were. We were prepared to enjoy a good meal. We reached Austin the next day. It was in the month of June. We suffered so much from the heat and felt so uncomfortable that we could not enjoy anything. We were glad to get started back to camp. Living in a higher altitude and in the open made us very sensitive to the heat.

Soon after our return to camp Captain Roberts made a business trip to Burnet. I accompanied him. We visited a favorite cousin of his, Mrs. J. A. Crews, who had a young lady living with her, Miss Nellie Mabry. She was a beautiful, accomplished girl; my guest chamber was vacant and I needed her. I described the delights of camp life in such glowing colors that she readily consented to accompany us home. When we drove into camp we could read expressions of pleasure on the Rangers' faces. They appreciated the fact that a pretty young girl was quite an acquisition to the Ranger camp. She enjoyed the novelty of camp life to its fullest extent. We fished and hunted. A Ranger was always ready to take us driving.

Nellie spent three months with us. When she returned home, she married the pastor of the Methodist Church at Burnet, notwithstanding I had told her my experience of a night spent at a preacher's house. There are preachers and *preachers*. The one she married was an intelligent, educated man. When I visited her, he was out preaching, but her larder was well filled. "In the good old days" ignorance and illiteracy were no bar to keep a man out of the pulpit if he imagined he had heard "the call." What a great change for the better has taken place.

The evening before Nellie left, we made a visit to the camp to say goodbye to the Rangers. We saw a bed ten feet long that attracted our attention and aroused our curiosity. They explained that while B. D. Lindsey was out on guard duty they had pieced his bed out to make it long enough for him. He stood six feet five inches in his stockings. He is now Captain Lindsey of San Antonio.

I mentioned the fact that Mr. Lindsey was on guard. Every morning several men were detailed to take the horses out to graze. At night only one man at a time was on guard. If he was caught napping he was dishonorably discharged. During the last few months that we were encamped on the San Saba the Indians made no raids into Menard County...

CAMP ON THE LLANO
NEAR JUNCTION CITY

Our camp was located in a beautiful live oak grove on the Llano River. The country is hilly. It was at that time on the extreme frontier. There were few settlements. There was not a fence in Kimble County. The first house to be built of lumber was on Farmer's Ranch, twenty miles above Junction. The lumber was hauled from Round Rock by ox teams.

The day before we reached our new camp four men were killed in Junction. I was very strongly impressed that we were in a bad man's country. My inclination to hunt and fish suddenly vanished. Camp appeared to me the safest place to stay. With Ranger protection I did venture to carry my laundry to Junction. I found it comprised a few log cabins, so frequently described as the home of the pioneer. On our way back to camp the boys told me that they had heard at the post office that the women washed on the banks of the river and that they had had several fights. It made me very uncomfortable to know that we were in a country where women fought. I renewed my determination to stay close in camp and to take up my embroidery to pass the time.

A few days later I accompanied the Rangers, who were going after the mail, to bring back my laundry. I got out at the house where I had left the clothes; the Rangers went on to the post office. I walked boldly to the door, I might say fearlessly, without any premonition of the danger to which I was exposed. There were three women present, and as soon as I looked at them I saw their belligerent attitude. I was so taken by surprise that my voice may have trembled when I asked for my clothes. They said the clothes were washed, but that they would never wash for me again. Then they began to tell me their opinion of people who thought themselves better than other folks. They told me that they had been well raised, had always kept the best company, and continued for some time to pour forth a tirade of abuse, mixed with swear words, about stuck-up people. Money, they said, doesn't make any-one better.

During all this time I had not said a word. I could think of nothing to say that would save me. But when they spoke of money, I said, "Surely, you are not mistaking us for rich people. Rangers are all poor." On hearing my reply they were mollified. There was a great change in their manner. They as-sumed a friendly attitude, and one of them asked me to have a "chaw." That placed me in an awkward if not dangerous di-lemma. I was afraid to refuse for fear of giving offense. At that moment the Rangers drove up. I declined with thanks. I was glad to get back to camp. Later I learned that I had offended these women by not inviting them to visit me when I took the laundry down.

For nearly two weeks I stuck to my resolution to stay in camp, but the monotony of camp and the tempting attractive-ness of the Llano River caused me to waver. I took my gun and went back to hunting and fishing, which were fine. Company could not be had. Girls were scarce, and my acquaintance was limited.

Life was not monotonous for the Rangers. While the Indians had ceased to raid in Menard, they continued to dep-redate in Kimble. Besides hunting Indians, there was much police duty. We were not only in an Indian country, but also

in the country of the bad man. The Rangers were continu-
ally making arrests, and invariably they would be cussed out
by the wives. When the Rangers planned to make an arrest,
they took station near the suspect's house the night before,
and rushed upon it about daylight next morning before the
culprit would have time to escape.

The Rangers told the following joke on Captain Roberts.
The Captain opened a door just as day was breaking; he didn't
knock, and entered without ceremony. When he opened
the door the wife confronted him. He said, "Good morning,
Madam." She said, "Good morning, the devil!" and began
cursing him and his Rangers. It was not a pleasant business.
There was no jail in Kimble County; prisoners were taken to
Mason.

Some time after we had established ourselves on the Llano,
a report was brought to camp that a number of Indians had
been discovered on a mountain two miles distant. Sergeant
Sieker quickly formed a detail of ten men. The whole camp
was in a state of excitement. When Doug Coalson learned that
he was left off the detail, he came to our camp at top speed and
asked Captain Roberts to let him go. He had a special reason
for wanting a scalp. The Captain gave his permission. But in
a short time the detail return crestfallen. Someone must have
had double vision, for the mustangs were riderless.

Doug Coalson was a fine young man, and was one of our
best Rangers. His special reason for seeking revenge on the
Indians resulted from the murder of his two sisters and step-
mother. Doug's father was a hunter; it was the only occupation
in which he engaged. Hunting required that he live far from
the settlements. He did not like neighbors. When a family
moved within ten miles of his camp, he claimed that he was
being crowded out, and proceeded to move further on. He

provided his family with guns and ammunition. Mrs. Coalson was a good shot, and her boys Doug and Billie learned to shoot at an early age.

While the family was living on the Copperas, a small tributary of the Llano, Harris and his wife lived with them. Harris tried to farm. One morning about ten o'clock Mrs. Coalson saw fifteen Indians coming toward the house. Harris was in the field. Mrs. Coalson put on a man's coat and hat and walked out into the yard, hoping that the Indians would take warning that there was a man about the house. However, they continued to advance. She re-entered the house, and hung a quilt over the entrance, for there was no door or windows. Cracks between the logs furnished portholes through which to shoot. She gave each boy a gun, with orders not to shoot until she told them. The boys were ten and twelve years of age. When Harris saw the Indians, he ran toward the house, and arrived there at the same time with the Indians. He called for his gun, but fell before it could be handed to him by Mrs. Coalson. Mrs. Harris screamed when she saw her husband fall. Mrs. Coalson warned her that if she made any more noise she would have to knock her down with her gun, for she was trying to save her family. The Indians, emboldened by the woman's screams, started to enter the house.

Mrs. Coalson killed the first one that approached the door. The Indians took their dead away, but remained in sight about two hours. Doug said he had a fine bead on an Indian's eye, but that his mother would not permit him to fire. She was afraid of wasting ammunition, for she did not know how long they would be there. I do not remember how far Doug had to ride to get help to bury the murdered man.

When Mr. Coalson returned, he found his family ready to move to Menard. The children were sent to school, and he returned to his hunting. A few years after these events Mrs. Coalson passed to the great beyond. Mr. Coalson married again. He had two little girls. His family lived far out beyond the settlements. There the wife and little girls were overtaken by Indians and murdered.

While in camp on the Llano, we were invaded by a pest called "Star boarders." Men would ride into camp, turn their horses out with the herd and settle down for an indefinite stay with us. They would stay until requested by the sergeant or captain to move on. Sometimes the request had to take the form of an order before it produced results.

While at Menard I made the acquaintance of Mrs. J. W. Mears, sister of the Sieker brothers, and a warm friendship sprang up between us. Mrs. Mears was an educated and accomplished lady. She was reared in Baltimore, and it was a great change from there to the frontier of Texas. The cabin home in which she lived was like others that I have described. But inside the cabin one found decorations of her handiwork and a daintiness that showed culture and refinement. When visitors called she welcomed them with as much cordiality as if her home were a mansion. She was noted for her hospitality. Her husband was engaged in ranching.

When the loneliness of camp became too great for me, Sergeant Sieker fetched his sister and her baby boy, six months old, for a visit. A baby in camp was an event, and he became the most popular person in it. And I enjoyed the company of both more than words can tell. Give a woman a chance to talk to a sympathetic listener about the things that interest her and she will be happy.

A few days after Mrs. Mears returned home, the Indians made a raid into Kimble County and stole some horses. Captain Roberts sent a detail of half the men in camp to a water hole thirty miles west of us, hoping to intercept them. But instead of leaving the country, the Indians hid in the cedar brakes waiting for an opportunity to secure more horses. When Captain Roberts discovered their trick, he took all the Rangers left in camp except two, the orderly sergeant and a private. The sergeant guarded the large camp, a Ranger guarded ours. We had a negro cook. He would not stay at our camp, thinking he would be safer in the main camp. My husband assured me that there was no danger, as the Indians would not attack the camp, but I did not share his feeling of security. How I wished that the Indians had made their raid while Mrs. Mears was my visitor! After a few days Captain Roberts and the Rangers returned. They secured the horses, but the Indians got away. After their first encounter with the Rangers, the Indians did not stop to renew their acquaintance. My negro cook returned to Austin at the first opportunity.

Captain Roberts had business at Burnet. I was glad to accompany him and visit our cousin there. Some of the stage robbers that the Rangers had arrested were in jail at Burnet. Captain Roberts found that he would have to return at the end of a week when court opened. I remained in Burnet until he returned. He had to bring to Burnet a couple of women who were wanted as witnesses. My cook, a white man, told me the following joke on Captain Roberts: The evening before he was to start for Burnet, the Captain took the two women witnesses to camp. After supper he gave them some blankets and told them to occupy the vacant tent. As soon as Captain Roberts went to the main camp, the women began to investigate. They opened our tent and decided to occupy it. They said the damned captain could sleep on the blankets; and when he returned he found his bed occupied.

Captain Roberts and I were invited to attend a barbecue at
Menard on July 4th. As Menard was distant a day's drive, we
started on the 3rd, accompanied by two Rangers. We looked
forward with a great deal of pleasure to this meeting with our
friends. When we had gone about half way, we met a man riding at full speed, hatless, and so excited that he could scarcely
speak. He told us that about two miles back he counted fifteen
Indians. The Rangers with us were at once dispatched to camp
with orders to the sergeant to detail fifteen men. We followed
them, driving mules. It seemed to me that we would never
get to camp. After we met the detail I felt safe, for they were
going in the direction of the Indians. The Rangers returned
about night. They had trailed a bunch of mustangs. That was
another case of double vision...

REUNION

[After Captain Roberts tendered his resignation in 1882, he and his wife relocated to New Mexico. In his writing, he gives her health as the primary reason for leaving Texas. She gives no specific reason in hers. They returned to Texas after thirty years in New Mexico and in 1924 attended the Rangers reunion held at Menard.]

We returned to Texas to pass the remainder of our days in our beloved State. The old Texas Rangers had formed an association and were holding annual reunions. The next reunion would be held at Menard. We were delighted to have this opportunity of meeting the former Rangers, and particularly were we pleased that the reunion was to be held at Menard, our old stamping ground. The reunion was held about the last of August. We traveled from Austin to Menard in an auto in a few hours—a trip that in the "good old days" required four days. We arrived after dark. The next morning showed us a town of twenty-five hundred to three thousand inhabitants, with beautiful modern homes. We were the guests of Mr. and Mrs. W. W. Lewis. He was a young man and a member of our company when we last saw him. He is now a grandfather, and, in the words of Commander Green, "a prince among men."

The old Rangers had inaugurated these reunions about ten years ago. Major Green was elected commander and has been re-elected at each annual reunion. The meeting lasted three days, and everything was done for our entertainment.

Nowhere else are Rangers more highly appreciated than at Menard. The citizens said many nice things about the Rangers, and how greatly they were obliged to them for making the country safe for them to reside there. They are truly a generous and hospitable people.

Such a place and such people were ideal to recall the events of former times and renew friendships of days long ago. Only many of our friends and former Rangers had passed away. Indeed, on every hand were evident the great changes that time had wrought. Instead of the boyish faces of the Rangers we had left behind in the service, we were greeted by old men. Instead of seeing the pretty girls pictured in our memories, we met mature women surrounded by families. "Time and tide wait for no man." Time certainly does not wait, and it leaves its impress on man. One of the entertainments given the old Rangers was a dance. Some of us had never seen modern dancing. An old Ranger who sat by Captain Roberts was very much shocked, and as the dance progressed kept remarking to the Captain, "Now ain't that scandalous?"

Music and songs and the old-time ballads, varied the program. Mrs. Mears and another lady, whose name I cannot recall, played a piano duet that was very much appreciated. The reunion closed all too soon for us all.

On the morning following the close of the reunion, we were seated in the car with our nephew, Mr. W. H. Roberts, ready to return to Austin, when some of our friends took us out of the car and insisted that we remain longer. We spent two weeks delightfully. We were the guests of Mr. and Mrs. Lewis, but visited around with other friends. Once more we fished in the San Saba. We visited the old camp below Fort McKavett. We found the old fort in ruins. Near Menard we found the house still standing where we had spent our honeymoon. It was now used to store hay. Mrs. Ben Ellis, Mrs. Noguess and others surprised and honored us with a beautiful luncheon on the forty-ninth anniversary of our wedding.

The next two meetings of the Rangers Association were held at Ranger. We did not attend these. But the third year the meeting was again held at Menard. In the meantime he Baptists had established an encampment in a beautiful pecan grove. They placed the entire encampment at the service of the old Rangers. For the sake of "auld lang syne" we stopped at the Nimitz Hotel, but it was so modern that there was very little left that was familiar. At Menard we were the guests of Mr. and Mrs. Ed Mears during the reunion. Mr. Mears is a prominent cattleman. I had seen Ed before, with his mother he spent some time in camp when he was a baby. But I would never have recognized him again; he had changed so much. He has two daughters that are married. All of which raised the question in my mind: "How old is Ann?"

At this reunion eleven members of Company D were present, and a picture of the group was made. Colorado City, the home of Major Green, commander, was selected as the place for the next meeting. The attentions paid the old Rangers, the hospitality and entertainments were equal to those of the preceding reunion. Mrs. Winn made the most beautiful address that was delivered at the reunion.

The Rev. Dr. George Truett of Dallas began a ten days' meeting at the Baptist tabernacle immediately after the close of the meeting of the Rangers. It was my privilege to attend these meetings. We were the guests of Mrs. Ben Ellis. Again we visited the places that reminded us of the long ago, fished in the San Saba, and visited friends. While visiting at Mr. and Mrs. Wheliss we received a message requesting us to be at Mrs. Ellis' at four o'clock that some friends might call to see us. As we drove up, we found a number of cars parked. Our hostess met us at the door. She gave me a thread and requested that I follow it to the end to see where it would lead me. I followed the thread through the double parlors to the center table, on which there was a vase, and in the vase was a bag of gold. It was a gift from our friends, who declared that not being orators able to tell us how much the country owed to our protection, they had resorted to acts, and hoped we would interpret them right.

Delicious refreshments were served, and a very pleasant evening was spent amid our generous and appreciative friends. Had it not been that our relatives lived in and near Austin, no place could have been a more attractive home to us than Menard, with its loyal friends and hospitable citizens.

www.ingramcontent.com/pod-product-compliance
Lightning Source LLC
Chambersburg PA
CBHW020337100426
42812CB00029B/3155/J